Miriam Potocky
Antoinette Y. Rodgers-Farmer
Editors

Social Work Research with Minority and Oppressed Populations: Methodological Issues and Innovations

Social Work Research with Minority and Oppressed Populations: Methodological Issues and Innovations has been co-published simultaneously as *Journal of Social Service Research*, Volume 23, Numbers 3/4 1998.

Pre-publication
REVIEWS,
COMMENTARIES,
EVALUATIONS . . .

"**T**his volume addresses a number of social work issues. It not only successfully brings together critical information for research with minority and oppressed populations, but in doing so covers a number of methodologies and procedures, mental health issues, and prevention. This work is important reading to researchers and social work students alike."

Kevin Corcoran, PhD, JD
Professor, Graduate School of Social Work
Portland State University
Portland, OR

More pre-publication
REVIEWS, COMMENTARIES, EVALUATIONS . . .

"**P**otocky and Rodgers-Farmer have edited . . . a wide collection of articles that afford the reader a view of innovative research approaches for studying important issues affecting multicultural populations. . . . Included in "minority and oppressed populations" are a broad range of issues and diversity of groups, such as persons with AIDS, low income urban adolescents, women of color, nonwhite ethnic elders, [and] African American children, to name a few. The inclusion of this broad range of population groups highlights the breadth of oppressed populations. It suggests that some developments in research approaches may be generalizable to many of these groups.

. . . No other collection has focused attention on thoughful new approaches in social work research, such that common threads across research questions and samples can be drawn. This collection . . . represents a combination of conceptual and empirical works that address all stages of the research process."

Rosina M. Becerra, PhD
Professor
UCLA Department of Social Welfare
School of Public Policy
& Social Research

The Haworth Press, Inc.

Social Work Research with Minority and Oppressed Populations: Methodological Issues and Innovations

Social Work Research with Minority and Oppressed Populations: Methodological Issues and Innovations has been co-published simultaneously as *Journal of Social Service Research,* Volume 23, Numbers 3/4 1998.

The *Journal of Social Service Research* Monographs/"Separates"

These books were published simultaneously as special thematic issues of the *Journal of Social Service Research* and are available bound separately. Visit Haworth's website at http://www.haworth.com to search our online catalog for complete tables of contents and ordering information for these and other publications. Or call 1-800-HA-WORTH (outside US/Canada: 607-722-5857), Fax 1-800-895-0582 (outside US/Canada: 607-771-0012) or e-mail getinfo@haworth.com

Social Work Research with Minority and Oppressed Populations: Methodological Issues and Innovations

Miriam Potocky
Antoinette Y. Rodgers-Farmer
Editors

Social Work Research with Minority and Oppressed Populations: Methodological Issues and Innovations has been co-published simultaneously as *Journal of Social Service Research,* Volume 23, Numbers 3/4 1998.

The Haworth Press, Inc.
New York • London

Social Work Research with Minority and Oppressed Populations: Methodological Issues and Innovations has been co-published simultaneously as *Journal of Social Service Research*, Volume 23, Numbers 3/4 1998.

The development, preparation, and publication of this work has been undertaken with great care. However, the publisher, employees, editors, and agents of The Haworth Press and all imprints of The Haworth Press, Inc., including The Haworth Medical Press and The Pharmaceutical Products Press, are not responsible for any errors contained herein or for consequences that may ensue from use of materials or information contained in this work. Opinions expressed by the author(s) are not necessarily those of The Haworth Press, Inc.

The Haworth Press, Inc., 10 Alice Street, Binghamton, NY 13904-1580 USA

Cover design by Thomas J. Mayshock Jr.

Library of Congress Cataloging-in-Publication Data

Social work research with minority and oppressed populations: methodological issues and innovations / Miriam Potocky, Antoinette Y. Rodgers-Farmer, editors.
     p. cm.
     "Has been co-published simultaneously as Journal of social service research, volume 23, numbers 3/4 1998."
     Includes bibliographical references and index.
     ISBN 0-7890-0396-1 (alk. paper)
     1. Social service–Methodology. 2. Social service–Research. 3. Social work with minorities.
I. Potocky, Miriam. II. Rodgers-Farmer, Antoinette Y.
HV40.S6196 1998
362.84'0072–dc21
                               97-51813
                               CIP

INDEXING & ABSTRACTING

Contributions to this publication are selectively indexed or abstracted in print, electronic, online, or CD-ROM version(s) of the reference tools and information services listed below. This list is current as of the copyright date of this publication. See the end of this section for additional notes.

- *Abstracts in Social Gerontology: Current Literature on Aging,* National Council on the Aging, Library, 409 Third Street SW, 2nd Floor, Washington, DC 20024

- *Applied Social Sciences Index & Abstracts (ASSIA) (Online: ASSI via Data-Star) (CDRom: ASSIA Plus),* Bowker-Saur Limited, Maypole House, Maypole Road, East Grinstead, West Sussex RH19 1HH, England

- *Behavioral Medicine Abstracts,* University of Washington Department of Social Work & Speech & Hearing Sciences, Box 354900, Seattle, WA 98195

- *caredata CD: the social and community care database,* National Institute for Social Work, 5 Tavistock Place, London WC1H 9SS, England

- *CNPIEC Reference Guide: Chinese National Directory of Foreign Periodicals*, P.O. Box 88, Beijing, People's Republic of China

- *Criminal Justice Abstracts,* Willow Tree Press, 15 Washington Street, 4th Floor, Newark, NJ 07102

- *Criminology, Penology and Police Science Abstracts,* Kugler Publications, P.O. Box 11188, 1001 GD Amsterdam, The Netherlands

- *Current Contents . . . . see:* Institute for Scientific Information

- *Family Studies Database (online and CD/ROM),* National Information Services Corporation, 306 East Baltimore Pike, 2nd Floor, Media, PA 19063

- *Gay & Lesbian Abstracts,* National Information Services Corporation, 306 East Baltimore Pike, 2nd Floor, Media, PA 19063

- *Human Resources Abstracts (HRA),* Sage Publications, Inc., 2455 Teller Road, Newbury Park, CA 91320

- *IBZ International Bibliography of Periodical Literature,* Zeller Verlag GmbH & Co., P.O.B. 1949, d-49009 Osnabruck, Germany

- *Index to Periodical Articles Related to Law,* University of Texas, 727 East 26th Street, Austin, TX 78705

(continued)

- *Institute for Scientific Information,* 3501 Market Street, Philadelphia, Pennsylvania 19104. Coverage in:
  b) Research Alerts (current awareness service)
  c) Social SciSearch (magnetic tape)
  d) Current Contents/Social & Behavioral Sciences (weekly current awareness service)

- *INTERNET ACCESS (& additional networks) Bulletin Board for Libraries ("BUBL"), coverage of information resources on INTERNET, JANET, and other networks.*
  - <URL:http://bubl.ac.uk/>
  - The new locations will be found under <URL:http://bubl.ac.uk/link/>.
  - Any existing BUBL users who have problems finding information on the new service should contact the BUBL help line by sending e-mail to <bubl@bubl.ac.uk>.
  The Andersonian Library, Curran Building, 101 St. James Road, Glasgow G4 0NS, Scotland

- *Mental Health Abstracts (online through DIALOG),* IFI/Plenum Data Company, 3202 Kirkwood Highway, Wilmington, DE 19808

- *National Clearinghouse on Child Abuse & Neglect,* 10530 Rosehaven Street, Suite 400, Fairfax, VA 22030-2804

- *NIAAA Alcohol and Alcohol Problems Science Database (ETOH),* National Institute on Alcohol Abuse and Alcoholism, 1400 Eye Street NW, Suite 600, Washington, DC 20005

- *PASCAL, c/o Institute de L'Information Scientifique et Technique,* Cross-disciplinary electronic database covering the fields of science, technology & medicine. Also available on CD-ROM, and can generate customized retrospective searches. For more information: INIST, Customer Desk, 2, allee du Parc de Brabois, F-54514 Vandoeuvre Cedex, France; http//www.inist.fr

- *Psychological Abstracts (PsycINFO),* American Psychological Association, P.O. Box 91600, Washington, DC 20090-1600

- *Social Planning/Policy & Development Abstracts (SOPODA),* Sociological Abstracts, Inc., P.O. Box 22206, San Diego, CA 92192-0206

- *Social Science Citation Index . . . . see:* Institute for Scientific Information

- *Social Work Abstracts,* National Association of Social Workers, 750 First Street NW, 8th Floor, Washington, DC 20002

- *Sociological Abstracts (SA),* Sociological Abstracts, Inc., P.O. Box 22206, San Diego, CA 92192-0206

(continued)

SPECIAL BIBLIOGRAPHIC NOTES

related to special journal issues (separates)
and indexing/abstracting

☐ indexing/abstracting services in this list will also cover material in any "separate" that is co-published simultaneously with Haworth's special thematic journal issue or DocuSerial. Indexing/abstracting usually covers material at the article/chapter level.

☐ monographic co-editions are intended for either non-subscribers or libraries which intend to purchase a second copy for their circulating collections.

☐ monographic co-editions are reported to all jobbers/wholesalers/approval plans. The source journal is listed as the "series" to assist the prevention of duplicate purchasing in the same manner utilized for books-in-series.

☐ to facilitate user/access services all indexing/abstracting services are encouraged to utilize the co-indexing entry note indicated at the bottom of the first page of each article/chapter/contribution.

☐ this is intended to assist a library user of any reference tool (whether print, electronic, online, or CD-ROM) to locate the monographic version if the library has purchased this version but not a subscription to the source journal.

☐ individual articles/chapters in any Haworth publication are also available through the Haworth Document Delivery Service (HDDS).

Social Work Research with Minority and Oppressed Populations: Methodological Issues and Innovations

CONTENTS

ABOUT THE EDITORS

Miriam Potocky, PhD, is Assistant Professor and Acting Coordinator of the doctoral program in the School of Social Work at Florida International University in Miami, Florida. Dr. Potocky teaches courses in research methodology, data analysis, and social work with immigrants and refugees. She is the author of numerous publications in such journals as *Social Work Research, Social Work,* and *International Social Work,* and has given presentations in the area of refugee economic integration as it relates to refugee resettlement policy. Dr. Potocky is a member of several national social work organizations, such as the National Association of Social Workers, the Council on Social Work Education, and the Society for Social Work and Research. Her research interests focus on multicultural and international social work, particularly on refugee issues.

Antoinette Y. Rodgers-Farmer, PhD, is Assistant Professor at Rutgers, The State University of New Jersey, School of Social Work in New Brunswick, where she teaches Human Behavior and the Social Environment and Psychopathology. Dr. Rodgers-Farmer has spoken at numerous national and international conferences and is a member of the Council on Social Work Education. Currently, she is conducting research in the areas of adolescent health, kinship care, and parenting behavior.

Foreword

Social work research about multicultural groups requires methodologies that can be adapted in the context of cultural interests and diverse points of view. There have been conceptual developments in social work practice about minority and oppressed populations in the past two decades; however, there have not been corresponding methodological innovations in social work research. Typically, new research knowledge has been introduced by social scientists, particularly by anthropologists, sociologists, and psychologists. The work by social work researchers, although an important step in knowledge development, pointed to the differences in demographic variables across minority groups and other oppressed populations, with very little insight into the reasons for those differences.

Gratifying to the social work profession is the fact that great advances in social work research methodology have been made in recent years. Undoubtedly, this is a reflection of the increased efforts and sophistication of social work practitioners and researchers in studying social work with minority and oppressed populations. *Social Work Research with Minority and Oppressed Populations: Methodological Issues and Innovations* contains a representative sampling of these new developments. The editors, Miriam Potocky and Antoinette Y. Rodgers-Farmer, have provided an important service for social work researchers. They have carefully abstracted from each of the articles in this special collection research principles that can be generalized across different multicultural groups; and, most important, they have suggested fundamental research questions that will advance further knowledge about working with minority and oppressed populations. The contents of the articles indicate new techniques and adaptations of existing research methods to diverse populations; included are methods for recruiting subjects, development of action re-

---

[Haworth co-indexing entry note]: "Foreword." Tripodi, Tony. Co-published simultaneously in *Journal of Social Service Research* (The Haworth Press, Inc.) Vol. 23, No. 3/4, 1998, pp. xiii-xiv; and: *Social Work Research with Minority and Oppressed Populations: Methodological Issues and Innovations* (ed: Miriam Potocky and Antoinette Y. Rodgers-Farmer) The Haworth Press, Inc., 1998, pp. xiii-xiv. Single or multiple copies of this article are available for a fee from The Haworth Document Delivery Service [1-800-342-9678, 9:00 a.m. - 5:00 p.m. (EST). E-mail address: getinfo@haworth.com].

search, sampling, a method for constructing interval scales, and conceptualizations for expanding factors in assessment as well as defining salient clinical constructs such as depression. Moreover, extensive bibliographic references and reviews of research are provided about gay and bisexual men, low-income urban adolescents, depressed women of color, ethnic elders, and African-American and white children.

This volume is must reading for social work researchers. Written by outstanding social work scholars, it provides key issues and conceptual challenges for research with minority and oppressed populations. Highly recommended for social work academicians, practitioners, administrators, policy developers, and students, it sensitizes readers to issues and suggestions for developing prevention programs and implementing social work interventions.

This is a gem of a volume. It is succinct, authoritative and of the highest quality. I learned a great deal from reading it. There is something of value here for all social workers. Although this is a slim volume, it is extremely thought-provoking and important for the advancement of the social work profession.

Tony Tripodi
President, Society for Social Work and Research
Dean, The Ohio State University College of Social Work

Introduction

Miriam Potocky
Antoinette Y. Rodgers-Farmer

During the past two decades there has been a vast increase in the social work literature in articles reporting on research with minority and oppressed populations. There has not, however, been a commensurate increase in literature that addresses the methodological challenges of and strategies for conducting such research. A few seminal articles in the social work literature (for example, Becerra & Zambrana, 1985; Lockhart, 1985; Myers, 1979; Wong, 1982) as well as recent publications in allied disciplines (for example, Eichler, 1988; Okazaki & Sue, 1995; Ponterotto & Casas, 1991; Smith & Madison, 1992; Stanfield & Dennis, 1993) have sensitized us to the need to adapt traditional research approaches when working with minority and oppressed respondents. Building on these as a foundation, the purpose of this special publication is to bring together in one volume a collection of articles that present state-of-the-art knowledge and techniques on this topic.

We invited leading social work scholars who are actively engaged in research with minority and oppressed populations to contribute to this volume. Of the abstracts received, we selected those that presented the most insightful conceptualizations of the relevant challenges, as well as the most innovative strategies for addressing those challenges. Additionally, we were interested in presenting research principles that are generalizable to a variety of minority and oppressed populations. We believe this volume will be useful to established researchers and graduate students

Address correspondence to Miriam Potocky, School of Social Work, Florida International University, 3000 NE 145th Street, ACI-234, North Miami, FL 33181 (e-mail POTOCKYM@SERVAX.FIU.EDU).

[Haworth co-indexing entry note]: "Introduction." Potocky, Miriam, and Antoinette Y. Rodgers-Farmer. Co-published simultaneously in *Journal of Social Service Research* (The Haworth Press, Inc.) Vol. 23, No. 3/4, 1998, pp. 1-3; and: *Social Work Research with Minority and Oppressed Populations: Methodological Issues and Innovations* (ed: Miriam Potocky, and Antoinette Y. Rodgers-Farmer) The Haworth Press, Inc., 1998, pp. 1-3. Single or multiple copies of this article are available for a fee from The Haworth Document Delivery Service [1-800-342-9678, 9:00 a.m. - 5:00 p.m. (EST). E-mail address: getinfo@ haworth.com].

who possess fundamental knowledge of basic issues pertaining to cross-cultural research, such as power and status considerations, biased problem definition, respondent mistrust, sampling error, and test bias.

The articles contained herein represent a combination of conceptual and empirical works that address all stages of the research process: conceptualization, operationalization, measurement, research design, data collection, analysis, and interpretation. The articles make several new contributions to the existing literature on this topic. Roffman et al. describe the use of anonymous enrollment as a technique for engaging and retaining respondents in research. While the use of anonymity per se is a common research technique for increasing the validity of responses, what is new in this case is the application of this method in the context of intervention research–that is, research that includes a direct service delivery component. Since direct interventions typically involve face-to-face contact, and since members of minority and oppressed groups underutilize such services, the anonymous enrollment technique holds promise for increasing access to "hidden" populations. Safyer et al. provide a detailed account of the process of conducting an action research project. Their report is particularly valuable in its focus on the developmental stage of the research, a phase which is too frequently omitted from research reports in favor of a decontextualized emphasis on outcomes. Both Ortega and Richey, and Burnette address issues involved in research with "dually oppressed" populations–ethnic minority elders and women, respectively. These two articles provide comprehensive and complementary perspectives on highly sophisticated approaches related to definitions, measurement, and the expansion of conceptual frameworks. Finally, DeRoos and Allen-Meares present a relatively unknown statistical technique, Rasch Analysis, as a method for discerning differences in the subjective experiences of depression by members of different racial groups, using the same measurement instrument.

Before the Summary of each article, we provide a brief review of the article in which we point out the generalizable research principles that can be derived from the work, as well as suggestions for future directions. We thank all of the contributors as well as David F. Gillespie, Editor, *Journal of Social Service Research*, for their hard work and patience in preparing this volume.

REFERENCES

Becerra, R. M., & Zambrana, R. E. (1985). Methodological approaches to research on Hispanics. *Social Work Research and Abstracts, 21*, 42-49.

Eichler, M. (1988). *Nonsexist research methods: A practical guide*. Boston: Unwin Hyman.

Lockhart, L. L. (1985). Methodological issues in comparative racial analyses: The case of wife abuse. *Social Work Research and Abstracts, 21*, 35-41.

Myers, V. (1979). Survey methods and socially distant respondents. *Social Work Research and Abstracts, 15*, 3-9.

Okazaki, S., & Sue, S. (1995). Methodological issues in assessment research with ethnic minorities. *Psychological Assessment, 7*, 367-375.

Ponterotto, J. G., & Casas, J. M. (1991). *Handbook of racial/ethnic minority counseling research*. Springfield, IL: Charles C Thomas.

Smith, N. L., & Madison, A. (Eds.) (1992). *Minority issues in program evaluation*. San Francisco: Jossey-Bass.

Stanfield, J. H., & Dennis, R. M. (Eds.) (1993). *Race and ethnicity in research methods*. Newbury Park, CA: Sage.

Wong, P. (1982). Social work research on minorities: Toward a comparative approach. *Journal of Education for Social Work, 18*, 69-76.

Anonymous Enrollment in AIDS Prevention Telephone Group Counseling: Facilitating the Participation of Gay and Bisexual Men in Intervention and Research

Roger A. Roffman
Joseph Picciano
Lauren Wickizer
Marc Bolan
Rosemary Ryan

EDITORS' NOTE. This article describes the use of anonymous enrollment as a technique for engaging and retaining respondents in research. The following generalizable research principles and directions

Roger A. Roffman, Joseph Picciano, Lauren Wickizer and Rosemary Ryan are all affiliated with the School of Social Work at the University of Washington. Marc Bolan is affiliated with the Department of Sociology, University of Washington.

The authors wish to express their appreciation to Dr. Blair Beadnell, Ms. Lois Downey, Mr. Douglass Fisher, Ms. Cher Gunby, and Ms. Lois Meryman for their assistance with this research.

This research was supported by grant MH 46792 from the National Institute of Mental Health, Bethesda, MD.

Address correspondence to Roger A. Roffman, School of Social Work, University of Washington, 4101 15th Avenue N.E., Seattle, WA 98105-6299.

[Haworth co-indexing entry note]: "Anonymous Enrollment in AIDS Prevention Telephone Group Counseling: Facilitating the Participation of Gay and Bisexual Men in Intervention and Research." Roffman, Roger A. et al. Co-published simultaneously in *Journal of Social Service Research* (The Haworth Press, Inc.) Vol. 23, No. 3/4, 1998, pp. 5-22; and: *Social Work Research with Minority and Oppressed Populations: Methodological Issues and Innovations* (ed: Miriam Potocky and Antoinette Y. Rodgers-Farmer) The Haworth Press, Inc., 1998, pp. 5-22. Single or multiple copies of this article are available for a fee from The Haworth Document Delivery Service [1-800-342-9678, 9:00 a.m. - 5:00 p.m. (EST). E-mail address: getinfo@haworth.com].

for future research can be derived from this work: (1) Anonymous enrollment is a feasible option that can serve as a "gateway" to engaging clients in more traditional service delivery and data collection procedures. The feasibility and outcome of this technique in longitudinal research with other minority and oppressed groups needs to be investigated. Specifically, the validity of the method in obtaining representatives of the target population needs to be assessed and compared with other techniques for accessing hidden populations, such as snowball sampling. (2) Anonymous enrollment can serve as a tool for identifying those subgroups within minority populations who are most at risk, allowing for the development of specifically targeted interventions for these subgroups. (3) Researchers need to be sensitive to subtle barriers to service access in addition to the more commonly known barriers such as logistical issues and staff-client ethnicity differences. Future research is needed regarding the identification of such barriers and the development of additional creative means for overcoming them. (4) Stage of readiness for change is increasingly being recognized by many researchers as a crucial variable in treatment outcome; therefore, it should routinely be included in intake assessments. The development and evaluation of intervention strategies that are specifically matched to each stage of readiness for change is an important area for future research.

SUMMARY. Participants in an outcome study of a 14-week AIDS prevention counseling intervention, delivered entirely by telephone, were able to enroll either confidentially or anonymously. Anonymous enrollees (27%) were more likely to be bisexual, in a primary relationship with a female, and closeted. They were less self-accepting of their sexual orientation, less acculturated in the gay community, and less likely to have close social supports for safer sex. They were less likely to have been tested for HIV antibodies or to have participated in risk-reduction programs despite reporting risk behaviors comparable to that of confidential participants. By the program's conclusion, most anonymous enrollees had provided their phone numbers or other personally identifying information. Participants who retained their anonymity throughout (10%) were less likely to complete treatment or follow-up assessments. The findings support the effectiveness of anonymous enrollment in facilitating the participation of potential clients and research subjects who might otherwise have remained unreached. *[Article copies available for a fee from The Haworth Document Delivery Service: 1-800-342-9678. E-mail address: getinfo@haworth.com]*

INTRODUCTION

Uneven Adaptation of Risk-Reduction Behaviors

Despite substantial success among gay and bisexual men in avoiding sexual behaviors that present risk of HIV transmission, the findings of numerous studies indicate that this adaptation to the AIDS epidemic has taken place unevenly among various subgroups in this population (Adib et al., 1991; Centers for Disease Control, 1994; Dean & Meyer, 1995; Ekstrand & Coates, 1990; Hoover, Munoz, Carey et al., 1991; Lemp, Hirozawa, Givertz et al., 1994; Osmond, Page, Wiley et al., 1994; Peterson, Coates, Catania et al., 1992; Roffman, Downey, Beadnell et al., 1997; Rosenberg, Biggar, & Goedert, 1994). Several models of risk-reduction interventions with men who have sex with men appear to be effective, at least in the short-term, in facilitating safer sexual behaviors (Coates, Faigle, Koijane et al., 1995; Kelly, St. Lawrence, Hood, & Brasfield, 1989; Roffman, Downey, Beadnell et al., 1997; Roffman, Stephens, & Curtin et al., in press; Valdiserri, Lyter, Leviton et al., 1989). However, it is likely that various types of barriers–cultural, psychological, and logistic–function as obstructions to the delivery of these services to persons continuing to engage in high-risk behaviors.

Barriers to Delivery of Prevention Supports

Needs of Subgroups Within the Population. Individuals who experience themselves as minorities within the larger population of men who have sex with men may feel apprehensive about the preparedness of prevention program staff and fellow clientele to understand and resonate to their unique circumstances. These minority subgroups might include adolescents or individuals who are older, men of color, HIV-positive individuals, and men who are bisexual. In addition to fearing that they may risk being misunderstood or judged, closeted individuals may not be willing to seek assistance in becoming sexually safer because they fear that disclosing their sexual orientation to service providers or other clients raises unacceptable risks of further disclosure. Some individuals may resist the role of client, particularly if the prevention service is perceived as more psychotherapeutic and less attuned to culturally consonant methods of obtaining supports from outside of the family structure (Lum, 1996). Additionally, potential clients may not seek help because they believe the program will not appropriately address issues concerning physical or sexual victimization, or alcohol or other drug dependence problems, phenomena that are often related to sexual behavior.

Logistical Impediments. The limited availability of gay-sensitive in-person risk-reduction supports, perhaps more common in rural and suburban areas, is clearly a major barrier. For some, geographic distance may entirely preclude receiving these services. Those who do not have access to a vehicle or public transportation, persons with mobility constraints, individuals with hearing or visual impairments, and persons with child care responsibilities may also experience major impediments to obtaining in-person prevention supports.

Barriers Associated with Professional Status. A gay man with high visibility in his community as an AIDS educator, a physician, a police officer, a teacher, a journalist, or member of some other profession might find it difficult to acknowledge to others that he is personally struggling with maintaining safer sexual behaviors. As a consequence, he may be more likely than those with less community visibility to avoid seeking the supports he needs to achieve and maintain risk-avoidant sexual behaviors. Ironically, the gay AIDS educator who faces this dilemma may find himself unable to seek and benefit from the very assistance that he is providing to others.

Reducing Barriers

Ultimately, the effective design and delivery of HIV prevention supports for all gay and bisexual men who need them will require a wide array of strategies in order to overcome an extensive and complex set of barriers. Modalities of delivering risk-reduction supports that are less psychologically or logistically demanding than those characterizing conventional in-person contexts may enhance their accessibility and acceptability to the members of specific subgroups. One such modality is service via the telephone.

Data pointing to the importance of developing such alternative modalities for delivering prevention supports were obtained in a 1987 needs assessment study conducted in Seattle, Washington. Publicity in local media invited adults who were concerned about not being able to avoid AIDS-risk sexual behaviors to telephone a university research office for an anonymous interview (Roffman, Gillmore, Gilchrist et al., 1990). Despite acknowledging their intense concern about their ongoing high risk behavior, a substantial minority of callers indicated that they would not participate in a face-to-face safer sex counseling program. The paradox was disturbing. Clearly, some alternative way of reaching and serving these individuals had to be developed.

With funding from the National Institute of Mental Health, the authors designed and assessed the effectiveness of a 14-session cognitive-behavioral group intervention, delivered entirely by telephone, and tailored for gay and bisexual males who sought support in becoming sexually safer. In addition to its delivery via the phone, toll-free access and the option to enroll anonymously were other key components designed to reduce barriers to enrollment.

Data supporting the efficacy of this intervention are reported elsewhere (Roffman, Picciano, Ryan et al., 1997). The purposes for the present paper are twofold: (1) to examine the extent to which the anonymous enrollment option facilitated participation by individuals who would presumably be difficult to serve due to several of the barriers noted above; and (2) to provide an assessment of the impact of this option on treatment completion and longitudinal data collection. Because many of the above-identified barriers to the delivery of HIV-prevention supports are also likely to obstruct service delivery and research with a wide variety of minority and oppressed populations, this innovative approach has considerable relevance in the health, mental health, and social services fields.

METHOD

Publicity and Eligibility Criteria

The project's publicity strategies, implemented during a recruitment period that lasted from April 1992 through December 1993, included advertising in the gay press, news coverage in the mainstream press, distributing materials to HIV testing centers and gay/lesbian/bisexual health and social service agencies, and mailing posters to gay bars and baths (see Fisher et al., 1996). The materials emphasized that individuals could choose to remain anonymous. To be eligible, men were required to be at least 18 years old and to have engaged in at least three instances of either unprotected anal or oral sex with another man in the preceding three months. Eligibility screening excluded individuals with current active psychotic symptoms, suicidal risk, severe substance use, or for requesting assistance outside of the scope of the project (e.g., suppressing desire for sex with other males).

Anonymous and Confidential Enrollment Options

After being given assurances of confidentiality of client information, potential participants were asked whether they would like to enroll confidentially or anonymously. Those who chose the confidential option were asked to provide an address to which written materials and incentive payments could be mailed. They were also asked for a phone number and instructions as to the type of message that could be left so that staff could contact them. Typically, clients were called to confirm their group placements and to remind them of data collection interview appointments. One individual, demonstrating a creative approach to masking the call's real purpose for anyone else who might hear the message, requested that staff say "This is Theresa calling from St. Mary's Church" as his cue to phone the project.

Clients who chose to enroll anonymously were asked to rent a postal box in a nearby post office. The anonymous enrollee was advised that he would need to provide documentation of his identity to the Postal Service, but could request that the project use a pseudonym when mailing materials to him at that address. He was asked to rent the postal box for an initial six-month period, and a money order for $17.50 was then mailed to him, with no name written on the payee line, to cover this cost. Postal boxes were subsequently used to send clients notifications concerning their treatment group beginning date, written materials, and incentive payments for completing post-treatment assessments.

Enrollment, Assignment, and Data Collection

During the enrollment period, 548 participants were randomly assigned to either treatment or a wait-list control condition. Those assigned to treatment were put into the next available counseling group and reassessed after their 14 weekly sessions were completed. Participants assigned to the control condition were reassessed 14 weeks later and then were offered the intervention. Experimental condition participants were reinterviewed at the three, six, and twelve month anniversaries of treatment completion.

Intervention

Telephone group sessions were conducted via teleconference bridge equipment that was purchased for the study. This equipment made it possible to merge as many as eight incoming calls without having to use the telephone companies for this purpose.

The 14-session intervention, based on Marlatt and Gordon's (1985) relapse prevention model, was gay-affirmative and sex-positive. The sessions focused on the development of group cohesion, HIV education, motivational enhancement, goal-setting, identifying antecedents to risky behavior, and developing effective coping strategies in dealing with high-risk situations so as to reduce HIV transmission vulnerability.

Each group, comprised of six clients, was co-led by male-female co-therapist teams. Session protocols, developed in previous pilot testing, described exercises to be used and provided guidelines for how much time should be devoted to each component.

Specific facets of the intervention were designed to address diversity in the intended service recipients. As an example, a compilation of reprinted articles focused on such issues as being a gay man of color, the older gay male, the coming out process, being closeted, and being HIV-positive. Participants were also asked to listen to a series of five 15-minute audiotaped discussions about safer sex by four men who represented varying races, serostatus, sexual orientation (i.e., exclusively gay and bisexual), and closetedness.

Measures

Demographic measures included age, ethnicity, income, and education. Participants were asked if they currently shared a committed relationship with a man and/or a woman. Ten items measured participants' agreement or disagreement (1 = strongly disagree to 4 = strongly agree) with possible reasons for favoring either an in-person or by-telephone method of delivering group counseling.

At baseline and each subsequent assessment, participants provided counts of their recent anal and oral penetrative sexual activities, and whether or not a condom was used. With reference to their sexual activities over the past year, participants were asked to rate on a five-point scale (1 = very low to 5 = very high) their risk of becoming exposed (or reexposed) to HIV.

Several items were used to measure sexual identity and preferences. Two 7-point Kinsey scales (exclusively homosexual to exclusively heterosexual) pertained to sexual orientation, one focusing on behavior and the other based upon feelings. Another item asked participants to identify the term they use when referring to their sexual orientation (e.g., gay, homosexual, bisexual, heterosexual, straight, no term, some other term). Seven items (1 = strongly disagree to 4 = strongly agree) focused on personal acceptance about being gay (e.g., "It's easy for me to accept that I have sex with men." "Having sex with men is a positive expression of sexuality."). A lower score was indicative of less acceptance. As an indicator of acculturation in the gay community, participants were asked to indicate which of twelve activities (e.g., subscribe to a gay newspaper, donate to a gay cause or organization) they had engaged in during the past five years.

Participants rated their level of closetedness on a five-point scale. They were also asked to indicate whether they had been tested for HIV antibodies and, if tested, their serostatus.

The social support measures pertained to the six persons in the participant's social network whom he thought of as the most important adults in his life. The participant was asked to identify each of these individuals by name or initials, and then to indicate each person's gender and sexual orientation, whether the person shared the participant's ethnicity, whether the person was aware of the participant's sexual orientation, whether he had discussed the topic of safer sex with this person, and the extent to which he viewed this network member as being accepting of the participant's sexual orientation (1 = not at all accepting; 5 = extremely accepting).

Six items focused on participants' perceptions of safer sex norms among their peers (i.e., complete acceptance of safer sex), and high risk behaviors engaged in (i.e., always using condoms with anal intercourse). A lower score on this five-point scale indicated the perception of less normative support for safer sex.

Participants were asked if they knew of specific safer sex supportive resources being available to them locally (e.g., counseling associated with HIV antibody testing, other safer sex counseling, a self-help group focusing on safer sex, or a workshop or class on safer sex). They were also asked if they had participated in each of these types of HIV-prevention services.

Data Analysis

Analyses were conducted to determine differences between anonymous and confidential enrollees in relation to the measures described previously and to intervention completion and follow-up participation. Because this study was the first to examine these issues, it was deemed important to identify as many potential differentiating variables as possible to guide further research. Therefore, bivariate analyses were conducted on multiple measures and items. It is recognized, however, that this approach increases the probability of obtaining significant results by chance.

RESULTS

Of 548 interested and eligible participants randomized to either the immediate treatment or wait-list control conditions, twenty-seven percent (N = 146) initially enrolled in the study anonymously. Over time, however, largely to enable the staff to make reminder calls of upcoming interviews or counseling group start dates, 92 of these individuals disclosed their telephone numbers, provided their residential addresses, or gave their full names. Thus, by the study's conclusion, nearly two-thirds (63%) of those who began as anonymous enrollees had disclosed personally identifying information. Only 54 individuals (10%) retained complete anonymity.

They were older (39.2 vs. 35.8 years of age; t[144] = 2.09, p < .05), more closeted (71.7% vs. 46.7%; χ^2[1, n = 145] = 8.50, p < .01), less likely to be exclusively gay based on the Kinsey behavior measure (27.8% vs. 51.1%; χ^2[1, n = 146] = 7.57, p < .01), and more likely to be in a primary relationship with a female (38.9% vs. 16.3%; χ^2[1, n = 146] = 9.34, p < .01) than those who eventually disclosed some aspect of their identity. They were also more likely to perceive themselves to be at a low risk of HIV transmission (72.2% vs. 49.5%; χ^2[2, n = 145] = 7.70, p < .05).

Baseline demographic characteristics, distinguishing between enrollees who selected the anonymous or confidential options at the time of their enrollment, are detailed in Table 1. These groups did not differ in terms of participants' age or race, with the average age of participants being in the mid-thirties and the majority being Caucasian. Those who chose to enroll anonymously were more likely to be college graduates and report an annual income of $20,000 or greater. The majority in both groups reported that they were not currently in a primary relationship with either a male or a female, although primary female relationships were more likely among anonymous enrollees (25% vs. 5%).

Detailed in Table 2 are data pertaining to a series of items which addressed potential reasons for favoring one or the other of two options for service delivery: counseling via the telephone or in-person. The percentages reflect answers indicating either agreement or strong agreement with each item. No differences were found on the first three items which pertained to the logistics and time demands of participating in an in-person program. However, anonymous enrollees were more likely to favor telephone-based services: not having to look at other people would make it easier to talk; the ability to participate without others knowing one's identity was valued; and there would be less concern about the possibility of meeting someone the person knew in a face-to-face group. Consistent with these answers, the anonymous enrollee was also less likely to endorse statements that: it would be harder to talk without seeing others' faces, and attending a face-to-face group would be preferable if one were available. Finally, a larger percentage of anonymous enrollees (39% vs. 20%) indicated that they would not participate in an in-person safer sex counseling group if that were their only option.

Sexual identity and closetedness, measures of acculturation within the gay community, and social supports also revealed differences between anonymous and confidential enrollees (Table 3). Anonymous participants were less likely to report exclusively gay behavior or feelings on the Kinsey scale items, or to self-label as gay or homosexual. A higher percentage of anonymous enrollees indicated that they were closeted, and

TABLE 1. Baseline Characteristics Among Anonymous and Confidential Enrollees

	Anonymous (n = 146)	Confidential (n = 402)
Demographics		
AGE		
18-24	6.8%	12.2%
25-29	20.5%	17.7%
30-34	16.4%	21.1%
35-39	17.8%	18.7%
40+	38.4%	30.3%
Average AGE	37.1	35.6
RACE		
Caucasian	78.1%	83.3%
Non-Caucasian	21.9%	16.7%
EDUCATION (highest level)*		
HS or Some Tech.	10.3%	14.9%
Some or 2 yr. College	31.5%	38.1%
College Grad or More	58.2%	47.0%
INCOME*		
Under $10,000	15.2%	19.4%
$10-19,999	10.3%	22.4%
$20-29,999	24.1%	24.4%
$30-39,999	22.8%	15.7%
$40-49,999	9.0%	8.2%
$50,000+	18.6%	10.0%
PRIMARY RELATIONSHIP WITH MALE		
No	82.1%	76.6%
Yes	17.9%	23.4%
PRIMARY RELATIONSHIP WITH FEMALE*		
No	75.3%	94.7%
Yes	24.7%	5.3%

*$p < .05$ based on Pearson Chi-Square

they had a significantly lower mean score on the seven self-acceptance items pertaining to being gay or bisexual.

Data from the 12 items measuring acculturation in the gay community indicated that anonymous participants were less likely than confidential enrollees to subscribe to gay publications, less likely to demonstrate social activism within the gay community (e.g., donate money, participate in marches, wear gay pride buttons or clothing, volunteer or do paid work for

TABLE 2. Reasons for Favoring Counseling via the Telephone or In-Person (percent agreeing or strongly agreeing) Among Anonymous and Confidential Enrollees

	Anonymous (n = 146)	Confidential (n = 402)
It's important to me that I don't have to travel somewhere to attend the group.	75.7%	68.6%
Having to drive a reasonable distance to attend the group wouldn't be a problem for me.	62.3%	68.3%
If I had to allow for travel time, I wouldn't be able to fit the group into my schedule.	43.4%	39.8%
The fact that I don't have to look at other people will make it easier to talk.*	64.1%	54.1%
I like that I can do this without anyone knowing who I am.*	85.6%	57.6%
If I had to attend a face-to-face group somewhere, I'd worry about running into people I know.*	58.2%	38.9%
It will be harder to talk when I can't see other people's faces.*	11.7%	19.3%
I'd prefer attending a face-to-face group if one were available.*	28.3%	48.7%
It seems less threatening to talk about safer sex on the phone than in person.	73.3%	67.0%
If my only option were in-person, I wouldn't join a group to talk about safer sex.*	38.9%	20.3%

*p < .05 based on Pearson Chi-Square

gay causes), and less likely to participate in gay social or cultural activities (e.g., go to bars or baths, participate in gay social events or activities, attend support or counseling groups for gay men, or use a gay computer bulletin board).

With reference to the six individuals identified by each participant as the most important adults in his life, anonymous enrollees reported a smaller percentage of these social network members who were gay, lesbian, or bisexual. Also, a smaller percentage knew of the participants'

TABLE 3. Sexual Identity and Acculturation in the Gay Community

	Anonymous (n = 146)	Confidential (n = 402)
Sexual Identity		
SEXUAL ORIENTATION (Behavior)*		
Not Exclusively Gay	57.5%	25.6%
Exclusively Gay	42.5%	74.4%
SEXUAL ORIENTATION (Feelings)*		
Not Exclusively Gay	68.5%	42.0%
Exclusively Gay	31.5%	58.0%
SEXUAL ORIENTATION (Labeling)*		
Gay or Homosexual	54.1%	83.9%
Bisexual	36.3%	12.7%
Straight	6.1%	0.2%
Other	3.8%	3.2%
CLOSETEDNESS*		
Definitely/Mostly In	55.9%	15.2%
50% or More Out	44.1%	84.8%
Sexual Preference and Identity Scale**		
(average)	2.88	3.35
Acculturation		
Sometimes reads gay newspaper	94.5%	97.5%
Has subscribed to gay newspaper*	16.4%	30.6%
Has donated money to gay causes*	50.0%	74.6%
Has participated in marches or demonstrations*	26.7%	51.7%
Has done paid or volunteer work for gay causes*	25.3%	55.7%
Has worn gay buttons, t-shirts, etc.*	24.7%	55.7%
Has gone to gay bars*	90.4%	95.5%
Has gone to gay baths*	43.8%	54.0%
Has participated in organizing gay social activities*	43.8%	60.9%
Has attended support or counseling groups for gay men*	37.7%	51.5%
Has attended gay cultural events*	40.4%	63.9%
Has used gay computer bulletin board*	12.3%	23.9%
Social Supports		
Percent of network who are gay*	35.5%	46.7%
Percent of network who know participant has sex with men*	53.3%	84.7%
Percent of network with whom participant has discussed safer sex*	46.4%	69.1%
Mean acceptance score of network re: participant's having sex with men*	3.18	3.88
Perceived Norms Scale (average)	2.73	2.76

*p < .05 based on Pearson Chi-Square
**p < .05 based on Independent Samples Student T-Test

sexual orientation. Anonymous enrollees reported conversations about safer sex with fewer of their network members. Finally, when compared with confidential enrollees, anonymous participants perceived members of their social networks to be less accepting of the participants' sexual orientation.

No differences were found between confidential and anonymous enrollees on the average scores of perceived norms for safer sex among gay and bisexual men known to the participants. Overall, participant scores suggested fairly weak normative supports for sexual safety.

With reference to recent sexual activity, there were no differences between the groups in terms of the percentages reporting one or more instances of unprotected oral or anal sex within the four weeks prior to baseline assessment (see Table 4). However, when the time period was expanded to 12 weeks prior to enrollment, fewer anonymous enrollees reported having engaged in unprotected anal sex during that period. In assessing their level of risk for being infected with HIV based on their sexual activities over the past year, anonymous enrollees rated themselves as at lower risk than did participants who enrolled confidentially.

With reference to the local availability of HIV-prevention supportive resources, there was no difference between groups: 72% of the anonymous participants and 79% of those who enrolled confidentially reported that at least some prevention services existed in their communities. Nonetheless, anonymous enrollees reported having previously participated in fewer HIV prevention activities. Specifically, they were less likely to have been tested for HIV antibodies and to have attended safer sex workshops. Anonymous enrollees reported previously utilizing fewer of the three types of HIV-prevention services overall.

Finally, the data in Table 5 illustrate the percentages of participants who completed the project's telephone intervention as well as of those who completed the various follow-up assessments. Unlike the previous tables, this table distinguishes between three groups of participants: those who retained their anonymity throughout the study, those who eventually converted from anonymous to confidential enrollment status, and those who began as confidential enrollees. Significant differences across the three enrollment categories were found for each of the measures: completed post/reassessment; completed counseling; and, completed 3, 6 and 12 month assessments, respectively. (The latter two measures pertain only to treatment group participants.) In addition, if the data are collapsed to specifically test differences between those who retained their anonymity throughout versus those who enrolled confidentially or converted to that status (data not shown explicitly), we find that participants who retained

TABLE 4. HIV Risk Behaviors and Prevention History

	Anonymous (n = 146)	Confidential (n = 402)
HIV-Risk Behaviors		
BEHAVIORS		
1+ Unprotected anal in prior 12 weeks*	42.5%	54.2%
1+ Unprotected anal in prior 4 weeks	31.5%	39.1%
1+ Unprotected oral in prior 4 weeks	92.5%	90.3%
HIV Prevention Resources		
HIV TESTED*		
No	19.2%	9.0%
Yes	80.8%	91.0%
HIV TEST RESULT (for those tested)*		
Positive	7.7%	19.8%
Negative	91.5%	79.1%
Don't Know	0.9%	1.1%
SERVICES AVAILABLE		
No	27.4%	21.2%
Yes	72.6%	78.8%
ATTENDED COUNSELING (if services available)		
No	74.5%	67.7%
Yes	25.5%	32.3%
ATTENDED SELF-HELP (if services available)		
No	77.4%	67.9%
Yes	22.6%	32.1%
ATTENDED WORKSHOP (if services available)*		
No	73.6%	60.1%
Yes	26.4%	39.9%
SERVICES USED (if services available)*		
none	50.9%	41.3%
one	30.2%	27.3%
two	12.3%	17.5%
three	6.6%	14.0%
SERVICES USED (if services available)**		
average number	0.75	1.04
CHANCE EXPOSED TO HIV*		
Low	57.9%	47.9%
Moderate	30.3%	31.8%
High	11.7%	20.3%

*p < .05 based on Pearson Chi-Square
**p < .05 based on Independent Samples Student T-Test

TABLE 5. Completion of Treatment and Follow-Up Assessments

	Anonymous (n = 54)	Anonymous to Confidential (n = 92)	Confidential (n = 402)
COMPLETED POST/REASSESSMENT*			
No interviews completed	61.1%	21.7%	22.4%
1-3 Interviews	5.6%	9.8%	7.2%
All 4 Interviews	33.3%	68.5%	70.4%
TREATMENT GROUP ONLY	(n = 33)	(n = 62)	(n = 245)
COMPLETED COUNSELING*			
No sessions attended	45.5%	8.1%	12.7%
1-9 sessions	36.4%	37.1%	33.9%
10+ sessions	18.2%	54.8%	53.5%
COMPLETED 3 MONTH ASSESSMENT*	15.2%	66.1%	73.5%
COMPLETED 6 MONTH ASSESSMENT*	18.2%	62.9%	71.4%
COMPLETED 12 MONTH ASSESSMENT*	18.2%	59.7%	68.2%

*p < .05 based on Pearson Chi-Square

anonymity were less likely to complete any of the four weekly post-treatment assessment interviews (38.8% vs. 77.7%; $\chi^2[1, n = 548] = 38.1$, p < .01). They were also less likely to complete treatment, defined as participating in 10 or more of the 14 sessions (18.2% vs. 53.7%; $\chi^2[1, n = 340] = 15.08$, p < .01).

DISCUSSION

The uneven and inconsistent adoption of safer sexual behaviors among a substantial percentage of men who have sex with men points to the need for innovative HIV prevention efforts. Key challenges to the field are identifying the factors that prevent the engagement in HIV-prevention counseling of individuals who are at high risk and developing effective means to overcome these obstacles.

This project sought to lower barriers to participant enrollment by delivering its counseling services and assessments completely by telephone, permitting access via a toll-free telephone number, and enabling participants to retain their anonymity if they wished. The findings support the effectiveness of the anonymous enrollment option in facilitating the participation in counseling of individuals who might otherwise have remained unreached. The method is, of course, limited to participants who have telephones and to interventions that can be adapted for delivery by telephone. The data also support the feasibility of anonymous enrollment of participants in longitudinal treatment outcome research.

Although a sizeable percentage of participants initially chose to enroll anonymously, presumably their evolving trust in the project's staff led to an eventual decision by many to provide personally identifying information. With only 10 percent of participants retaining anonymity throughout, the "costs" associated with their reduced likelihood of completing treatment and post-treatment assessments[1] appeared to have been outweighed by the "benefits" associated with this enrollment choice in terms of the project being able to reach many individuals at high risk of HIV transmission who otherwise would probably have been unserved. Nonetheless, a challenge for future researchers is to develop and assess more effective methods for delivering prevention supports to this select group of individuals. One possibility would be offering telephone counseling groups specifically for men who fit the profile of those who retained anonymity (i.e., older non-gay-identified men who have sex with men), and determining if this would enhance retention both in treatment and in subsequent follow-up assessments. Other programmatic components that might facilitate reaching this population are tailored marketing and an intake process that both acknowledges and sensitively deals with the caller's greater vulnerability to dropping out.

Clearly, these findings point to the advantages of permitting anonymous participation when seeking to overcome barriers to serving and conducting research with minority and oppressed populations. Whether the client's hesitancy to seek help or participate in research is based on distrust of providers' or researchers' motives, questions concerning the cultural competence of a program or its staff, uncertainty about becoming someone's client, ambivalence about initiating or reinitiating change, apprehension about disclosing sensitive and personal information, shame, low efficacy for succeeding with goals, anxiety about program fees and other costs, or any of a myriad of other barriers, knowing that one can remain anonymous offers a safety buffer that may greatly lower the risk in making an initial inquiry.

This study's finding that nearly two-thirds of those who initially enrolled anonymously eventually disclosed their identities suggests a potentially powerful modification for programs which now deliver only face-to-

---

1. Presumably, higher completion rates for confidential enrollees were somewhat a consequence of the staff's ability to follow up missed appointments and maintain closer contact with participants as needed.

face services to minority and oppressed populations. If one option for the new client included a period of service delivery via the telephone while retaining anonymity, the program's capacity to overcome the barriers listed above may be greatly enhanced. Clients who find that their initial positive experiences on the telephone effectively eliminate the concerns or fears that prevented them from making an in-person contact may subsequently choose to cross the agency's threshold. The anonymous enrollment option, when coupled with service delivery by telephone, thus may be one additional strategy for starting where the client is.

REFERENCES

Adib, S.M., Joseph, J.G., Ostrow, D.G., Tal, M., & Schwartz, S.A. (1991). Relapse in sexual behavior among homosexual men: A 2-year follow-up from the Chicago MACS/CCS. *AIDS, 5,* 757-760.

Centers for Disease Control and Prevention. (1994). US HIV and AIDS cases reported through June, 1994. *HIV/AIDS Surveillance Report, 6(2),* 10.

Coates, T.J., Faigle, M., Koijane, J. et al. (February, 1995). Does HIV prevention work for men who have sex with men? Report prepared for the Office of Technology Assessment, Congress of the United States.

Dean, L., & Meyer, I. (1995). HIV prevalence and sexual behavior in a cohort of New York City gay men (aged 18 to 24). *Journal of Acquired Immune Deficiency Syndromes, 8,* 208-211.

Ekstrand, M., & Coates, T. (1990). Maintenance of safer sexual behaviors and predictors of risky sex: The San Francisco Men's Health Study. *American Journal of Public Health, 180,* 973-977.

Fisher, D.S., Ryan, R.A., Esacove, A.W., Bishofsky, S., Wallis, M., & Roffman, R.A. (1996). The social marketing of Project ARIES: Overcoming challenges in recruiting gay and bisexual males for HIV prevention counseling. *Journal of Homosexuality 31,* 177-202.

Hoover, D.R., Munoz, A., Carey, V. et al. (1991). Estimating the 1987-1990 and future spread of human immunodeficiency virus type 1 in subgroups of homosexual men. *American Journal of Epidemiology, 134,* 1190-1204.

Kelly, J.A., St. Lawrence, J.S., Hood, H.V., & Brasfield, T.L. (1989). Behavioral intervention to reduce AIDS risk activities. *Journal of Consulting and Clinical Psychology, 57,* 60-67.

Lemp, G.F., Hirozawa, A.M., Givertz, D. et al. (1994). Seroprevalence of HIV and risk behaviors among young homosexual and bisexual men. The San Francisco/Berkeley Young Men's Survey. *Journal of the American Medical Association, 272,* 449-454.

Lum, D. (1996). *Social work practice and people of color: A process-stage approach* (3rd edition). Pacific Grove, CA: Brooks/Cole.

Marlatt, G.A., & Gordon, J.R. (1985). *Relapse prevention: Maintenance strategies in the treatment of addictive behaviors.* New York: Guilford Press.

Odets, W. (1994). AIDS education and harm reduction for gay men: Psychological approaches for the 21st century. *AIDS & Public Policy Journal, 9*, 1-15.

Osmond, D.H., Page, K., Wiley, J. et al. (1994). HIV infection in homosexual and bisexual men 18-29 years of age: The San Francisco Young Men's Health Study. *American Journal of Public Health, 84*, 1933-1937.

Peterson, J.L., Coates, T.J., Catania, J.A. et al. (1992). High-risk sexual behavior and condom use among gay and bisexual African-American men. *American Journal of Public Health, 82*, 1490-1494.

Prochaska, J.O., Velicer, W.F., Rossi, J.S., Goldstein, M.G., Marcus, B.H., Rakowski, W., Fiore, C., Harlow, L.L., Redding, C.A., Rosenbloom, D., & Rossi, S.R. (1994). Stages of change and decisional balance for 12 problem behaviors. *Health Psychology, 13*, 39-46.

Roffman, R.A., Downey, L., Beadnell, B., Gordon, J.R., Craver, J.N., & Stephens, R.S. (1997). Cognitive-behavioral group counseling to prevent HIV transmission in gay and bisexual men: Factors contributing to successful risk reduction. *Research on Social Work Practice, 7*, 165-186.

Roffman, R.A., Gillmore, M.R., Gilchrist, L.D., Mathias, S.A., & Krueger, L. Continuing unsafe sex: Assessing need for AIDS-prevention counseling. *Public Health Reports, 105*(2), March-April 1990, 202-208.

Roffman, R.A., Picciano, J.F., Ryan, R., Beadnell, B., Fisher, D., Downey, L., & Kalichman, S.C. (1997). HIV prevention group counseling delivered by telephone: An efficacy trial with gay and bisexual men. *AIDS and Behavior, 1*, 137-154.

Roffman, R.A., Stephens, R.S., Curtin, L., Gordon, J.R., Craver, J.N., Stern, M., Beadnell, B., & Downey, L. (in press). Relapse prevention as an interventive model for HIV risk-reduction in gay and bisexual men. *AIDS Education and Prevention.*

Rosenberg, P.S., Biggar, R.J., & Goedert, J.J. (1994). Declining age at HIV infection in the United States. *New England Journal of Medicine, 330*, 789-790.

Valdiserri, R.O., Lyter, D., Leviton, L., Callahan, C.N., Kingsley, L.A., & Rinaldo, C.R. (1989). AIDS prevention in homosexual and bisexual men: Results of a randomized trial evaluating two risk reduction interventions. *AIDS, 3*, 21-26.

Methodological Issues
when Developing Prevention Programs
for Low Income, Urban Adolescents

Andrew W. Safyer
Margaret L. Griffin
Neil B. Colan
Edith Alexander-Brydie
Janet Z. Rome

EDITORS' NOTE. This article reports on the developmental stages of an action research project (that is, research which actively involves the participants and other community members at all stages and which is designed to provide them tangible benefits). This portrayal of a work in progress illustrates the following generalizable research principles: (1) The developmental stage of an action research project is a long-term process, in this case, several years.

Andrew W. Safyer and Edith Alexander-Brydie are affiliated with the Boston University School of Social Work. Margaret L. Griffin and Neil B. Colan are affiliated with the Center on Work and Family, Boston University School of Social Work. Janet Z. Rome is affiliated with Boston Children's Services.

The authors gratefully acknowledge Cheryl Hyde, Leon Litchfield and Gail Stekettee for their helpful comments on an earlier draft of the manuscript and Cathie Rocheleau for her editorial assistance.

This study was supported by the Boston Foundation, Fidelity Foundation, Bank of Boston, and Boston University Medical Center.

Address correspondence to Andrew W. Safyer, School of Social Work, Boston University, 264 Bay State Road, Boston, MA 02215.

[Haworth co-indexing entry note]: "Methodological Issues when Developing Prevention Programs for Low Income, Urban Adolescents." Safyer, Andrew W. et al. Co-published simultaneously in *Journal of Social Service Research* (The Haworth Press, Inc.) Vol. 23, No. 3/4, 1998, pp. 23-46; and: *Social Work Research with Minority and Oppressed Populations: Methodological Issues and Innovations* (ed: Miriam Potocky and Antoinette Y. Rodgers-Farmer) The Haworth Press, Inc., 1998, pp. 23-46. Single or multiple copies of this article are available for a fee from The Haworth Document Delivery Service [1-800-342-9678, 9:00 a.m. - 5:00 p.m. (EST). E-mail address: getinfo@haworth.com].

23

Planning efforts need to take this into account. (2) Stakeholders (that is, the multiple constituents who will be impacted by the research) can and should be actively involved in needs assessment, program design and redesign, participant recruitment and retention, and evaluation design. Their involvement enhances access to respondents and increases the validity of the findings. The authors provide specific examples of how such involvement can be fostered. (3) Intakes into an intervention program should be staggered over time to allow for evaluation of the impact of programmatic changes. (4) Finally, as noted by these authors and others in this volume, conceptual frameworks should include "protective" and "strengths" factors as well as "risk" and "needs" factors.

SUMMARY. Project Opportunity is a prevention program for low-income, urban adolescents. It tests an innovative conceptual model that utilizes the workplace both to access teens who are dependents of low-wage employees and to provide services to the youths and parents at the site. Methodological lessons learned from implementing the Project are presented. Research considerations in selection of subjects, measures, and procedures must be adapted to match the specific challenges facing these families. Additional considerations not typically reported are critical, including establishing credibility among the various constituents, negotiating for access to families, and building staff commitment to an evaluation. *[Article copies available for a fee from The Haworth Document Delivery Service: 1-800-342-9678. E-mail address: getinfo@haworth.com]*

Adolescents growing up in low-income, urban families live in neighborhoods that are increasingly characterized by high rates of poverty, unemployment, inadequate health care, and unsupervised activities during the after-school hours (Carnegie Foundation, 1992; Garbarino, Dubrow, Kostelny, & Pardo, 1992; Gibbs, 1988; Prothrow-Stith, 1991; Richters & Martinez, 1993). Moreover, the rapid rise of violence in these neighborhoods jeopardizes the safety of adolescents (Gibbs, 1988; National Research Council, 1993). A disproportionate share of these youths have the added strain of minority status with the related experiences of racism and discrimination (Prothrow-Stith, 1991; Spencer & Dornbush, 1990). These environmental stressors place low-income, urban adolescents at risk for a variety of difficulties including substance abuse, depression, aggressive behavior, and school failure (Carnegie Foundation, 1992; Dryfoos, 1990; Prothrow-Stith, 1991).

While there is emerging interest in responding to the developmental needs and unique stressors of this population, such intervention programs are often plagued with methodological problems at every stage of the research process, including the development of the conceptual framework of the proposed project, the negotiations within the community required to implement the program, and the evaluation of the effectiveness of the program. This paper will present some lessons learned from *Project Opportunity*, a prevention program initiated by the Center on Work and Family at the Boston University School of Social Work, and Boston Children's Services. Since we view this prevention program as a demonstration project, a strong evaluation component is included. To date, program design, initial site selection, partial funding, and focus group activities of the Project have been completed (see Phases I-II following). A pilot program and a needs assessment survey have been completed and selection of additional sites and funding sources and a larger trial with 100-150 adolescents are ongoing (see Phases III-IV following).

Project Opportunity was designed to promote healthy development in economically-disadvantaged early adolescents and strengthen their relationships with their families and their neighborhoods. It also tests an innovative conceptual model that employs a risk and protective framework for problem behaviors and utilizes the workplace *both* to access teens who are dependents of low-wage employees and to provide services to the youths and parents at the worksite. The total length of the program is one year for each family, with adolescents participating in career mentoring activities, and in family support and education groups and community service activities with their parents (Safyer, Velez, & Colan, 1994).

PHASE ONE: DEFINING THE PROGRAM

A critical first step was developing an appropriate theoretical framework to guide program development. An emerging body of theoretical and empirical literature addresses the needs of urban, economically disadvantaged adolescents and their families, and discusses the implications of this information for prevention programs (e.g., Dryfoos, 1990; Safyer, 1994; Weissberg, Caplan, & Harwood, 1991). The following key ingredients, based on this literature, formed the conceptual framework of Project Opportunity: (1) targeting early adolescents; (2) identifying risk and protective factors for problem behaviors; (3) addressing risk and protective factors through a comprehensive, multiservice intervention program; (4) evaluating the program; and (5) utilizing the workplace as an alternative way to access hard-to-reach urban families and to provide services for them on site.

Targeting Early Adolescents

Research suggests that prevention programs need to be implemented during the early adolescent years when youth are less likely to be engaged in problematic behaviors (Carnegie Foundation, 1992). Early adolescence is a critical point in an individual's life trajectory due to the convergence of considerable physical, cognitive, and psychosocial forces (see Feldman & Elliot, 1990, for review). Successful adaptation to these demands is critical in ascertaining whether problematic behaviors will emerge in later life (Caplan & Weissberg, 1989). While this developmental transition is seldom smooth and straightforward, only 10-20% of teenagers from economically privileged backgrounds develop significant emotional or behavioral problems (Dryfoos, 1990; Hauser & Bowlds, 1990). The figure is believed to be higher among economically-disadvantaged urban adolescents (Carnegie Foundation, 1992; Dryfoos, 1990). These adolescents are more likely to be unsupervised during the after-school hours and are more likely to be exposed to illegal activity and chronic violence within their neighborhoods, as well as to have fewer social resources (Barone, Weissberg, Kasprow et al., 1995; Compas, Hinden, & Gerhardt, 1995; Garmezy, 1993; Haggerty, Sherrod, Garmezy, & Rutter, 1994; Luthar, 1993).

Identifying Risk and Protective Factors

Not all urban early adolescents, however, experience maladaptive developmental outcomes. Most of these youngsters are able to negotiate important developmental tasks and to use personal and social resources to achieve positive adaptational outcomes (Kazdin, 1993). Researchers have begun to identify those *protective factors* within individuals and their environments that either encourage successful development or shield adolescents from the *risk factors* that might hinder development (Dryfoos, 1990; Jessor, 1993; Kazdin, 1993). The identification of risk and protective factors influencing inner-city youth is emerging within the multiple domains of development: individual, family, peers, school, community, and society (Hauser & Bowlds, 1990; Jessor, 1993; Kazdin, 1993). Project Opportunity focuses on three of these domains: the individual, the family, and the community.

Addressing the Risk and Protective Factors Through a Multicomponent Program in Three Domains

In the past, prevention efforts have focused almost exclusively on implementing relatively circumscribed, single-component, short-term programs

(Small, 1990a; West, Aiken, & Todd, 1993). Given the environmental stresses related to poverty and the limited opportunities facing low-income, urban families, researchers have suggested that effective programs have multicomponent strategies to reduce risk factors and increase protective factors spanning several domains (Barone et al., 1995). Project Opportunity addresses multiple risk and protective factors at the individual, family, and community levels through career mentoring, family support and education, and community service activities, as shown in Table 1.

These particular interventions were chosen because the literature suggests they are particularly promising paths to achieving our goals. Career mentorships have been successfully implemented for low-income, urban adolescents (Funkhauser, 1993; Jobs for the Future, 1993). They reduce problematic behaviors, promote academic and social efficacy, and enable adolescents to establish meaningful relationships with adults (Funkhauser, 1993; Hamilton, 1990; National Research Council, 1993). Family support and education programs are seen as a promising approach to reduce substance abuse and other problem behaviors among adolescents and promote parenting skills and a positive family environment (Nelson, 1989; Small, 1990a; Weiss & Jacobs, 1988). While many programs target the parent, Project Opportunity brings adolescents and parents together to promote the development of such issues as open communication, and effective family coping skills (Colan, Mague, Cohen, & Schneider, 1994; Safyer et al., 1994). Community service programs have been shown to increase adolescents' feelings of responsibility and connection to their neighborhoods (Calabrese & Schumer, 1986; Hamilton & Fenzel, 1988; National Research Council, 1993), as well as to offer a meaningful alternative to substance use and other problem behaviors (Carnegie Foundation, 1992; Schinke & Gilchrist, 1985).

Each of these components has distinct goals. The goal of the *career mentoring component* is to give youngsters opportunities to learn about the technical and social aspects of a particular career, through "job shadowing" and appropriate "hands-on" experience-based activities. Participants interact with volunteer mentors and other adults in the workplace one or two afternoons each week.

The goal of the *family support and education component* is to strengthen neighborhood support networks, teach families specific skills for better managing family life, and provide leadership training for parents in advocacy issues for and with youth (Small, 1990a). It recognizes that families have strengths and skills that they bring to these meetings. Families meet in groups of approximately ten teens with their parents, once each month for two hours, in a workshop format which is alternately didactic and

TABLE 1. Risk and Protective Factors for Problem Behaviors by Domain and Matching Intervention

	INTERVENTION		
FACTOR	Mentoring	Family Ed	Community Service
I. Individual domain			
Risk factors			
Problem behaviors	X	X	X
Low self-esteem	X	X	X
Lack of supervision	X	X	
Protective factors			
Academic & social efficacy	X	X	X
Positive connections	X	X	
Involvement in safe haven activities	X	X	X
II. Family domain			
Risk factors			
Problem behaviors		X	X
Negative family environment		X	X
Lack of a natural support system		X	X
Protective factors			
Parenting skills		X	
Advocacy skills		X	
III. Community domain			
Risk factors			
Negative community perceptions			X
Lack of community involvement			X
Protective factors			
Community/cultural pride		X	X
Access to community role models		X	X
Knowledge of & access to community resources		X	

experiential in nature. Topics covered include parent-child communication, anger management, non-violent conflict resolution, advocating for teens in school, substance abuse education, and other topics generated by the families participating.

The goal of the *community service component* of the Project is to provide adolescents and their parents with regular opportunities to interact socially with one another and to strengthen their involvement with their communities. Once a month, during a weekend, adolescents and their parents participate in a community service project such as tutoring young children or serving at a soup kitchen, to enable participants to learn about and serve their neighborhoods and to address local problems.

Evaluating the Program

Since there have been few high quality evaluations of programs targeting low-income, urban adolescents and their families, documenting the effectiveness of Project Opportunity is an important contribution to those who wish to serve this population (Wilson-Brewer, Cohen, O'Donnell, & Goodman, 1991). In this era of shrinking federal and state funding for social programs, prevention efforts must be specific and well-informed to be plausible to funders (Small, 1990a). Some outcome evaluations have been supported, but many have very limited budgets, since funders prefer to focus on service delivery (Jacobs, 1988; Small, 1990b). Unfortunately, federal and private funding agencies typically overlook the importance of a process evaluation as an integral part of a successful demonstration project. The evaluation of Project Opportunity will include both outcome and process measures, and will address the inherent tension that exists between the desire to maintain scientific rigor in the evaluation process and the reality of conducting research in natural settings (Weiss & Jacobs, 1988).

Utilizing the Workplace to Reach Low-Income Urban Families

Prevention programs must also explore alternative ways to access low-income, hard-to-reach families. Traditionally, prevention programs have been offered at schools and other community-based organizations, such as youth centers (Carnegie Foundation, 1992). The changing nature of family life, such as the increase in dual-earner and single-parent families, often hinders access to these services (Felner, Brand, Mulhall et al., 1994; Safyer, Litchfield, & Leahy, 1996). While these changes affect most parents, they are especially problematic for families with fewer social resources. These families have limited non-work hours and would have to overcome obstacles, such as personal fatigue and other family concerns, to attend prevention programs (Felner et al., 1994). To address this issue, Project Opportunity accesses adolescents through their parents' place of employment and provides services to them on site. We do not know of any other workplace prevention program that targets employees and their adolescents.

PHASE TWO: PLANNING THE PROGRAM

Implementing the interventions derived from the conceptual framework outlined above necessitated establishing links in the community. This was critical for conducting the study but was especially important given our target population. In order to enhance credibility among constituents and to create a program responsive to the needs of the participants, Project Opportunity chose to use a practitioner-researcher partnership model (Hess & Mullen, 1995). This model is based on the belief that a collaborative relationship between researchers and practitioners is mutually beneficial. We extended this idea to include program participants plus all other collaborators identified as program constituents: mentors, workplace supervisors, community service agencies, additional family members of participants, the family education presenters, and a Steering Committee.

In practice, this model led us to interview the various constituents about their initial perceptions of the Project and any changing views of its strengths and weaknesses in operation. Participants' views were elicited most frequently, as described below. Feedback was then used to make adjustments to the program design, implementation, and evaluation. Credibility of the Project is enhanced by this model, as is its reliability and validity in the local and scientific communities.

During this phase, the following activities were implemented: (1) establishing a partnership with a local community agency, (2) creating a community-based Steering Committee to assist in conducting the Project, (3) locating potential business sites, (4) securing financial resources, (5) conducting focus groups and a community needs assessment survey, and (6) developing outcome measures.

Forming a Partnership with a Community Service Agency

Recognizing the value of a partnership with a social service organization that has extensive practice experience with urban, low-income families, representatives from the Center on Work and Family met with staff at Boston Children's Services, a well-established and well-respected organization. We felt this would increase the credibility of the Project with the target population. Boston Children's Services had recently developed a successful school and community partnership for low-income, urban youth that had convinced them of the effectiveness of working collaboratively with other organizations. They were particularly attracted to this Project for several reasons. It offered the potential to gain expertise in an underutilized social environment–the workplace. In addition, they believed that aligning themselves with a major research university would assist their efforts to compete for limited resources and increase their status within the social service community.

Developing an organizational structure for Project Opportunity that reflected the partnership model through sharing oversight between the two organizations necessitated many discussions over several months. Ultimately, the Center on Work and Family became responsible for the day-to-day management of the overall Project, including grant and budget management and supervision of key personnel, and for an evaluation of the Project. Boston Children's Services became responsible for the implementation and management of the various program activities.

Establishing a Steering Committee

While the lead organizations initiated the Project, we were interested in establishing a collaborative group that included a broad range of constituents to guide the implementation of the Project. After consulting with community leaders, Project staff from other local prevention programs, potential funders, and local community leaders, a Steering Committee was formed to provide guidance to the overall Project. Representatives of all constituents were appointed to the committee, including Project staff, participants, funders, community leaders, and workplace personnel. This organizational structure was one way of assuring that the core content of programs came from *within* the community and was not *dictated* by outside experts.

Initially, some community leaders were hesitant to join the Steering Committee. These individuals had mixed experiences with demonstration projects, especially those initiated by large research-based institutions which failed to acknowledge and validate the systems that were already operating in the community. It was their experience that these projects departed quickly after the program ended, without leaving tangible benefits for the community. Project staff addressed their concerns by outlining the active role members would play in shaping the final design of the program and by developing a plan to sustain the program after the initial funding portion had ended. In addition, the recruitment of the Steering Committee members was facilitated by the hiring of a new Project coordinator, a well-respected African-American woman with considerable visibility in the Boston social services community.

Despite the obvious appeal of including all constituents in a participatory organizational structure, some obstacles to their collaboration quickly became apparent. For example, while Steering Committee members expressed initial interest in the evaluation process, the meeting agendas allowed little group time for careful attention to evaluation issues. For this reason, a subcommittee of interested Steering Committee members and Project staff has been formed to focus on specific tasks, such as careful review of the survey items, and the development of new instruments.

Locating Potential Business Sites

At this stage of the Project development, we were interested in obtaining the commitment of two major corporations that had facilities in low-income Boston neighborhoods and employed a significant number of residents from the surrounding neighborhoods. We needed access to potential participants as well as internal support for conducting the study. Gaining access to potential business sites was challenging. Many companies have become overwhelmed by requests from community-based programs, because of calls for corporations to be "good citizens" by filling in some of the resource gaps created by cuts in federal and state programs (Googins, Hudson, & Pitt-Castouphes, 1995).

Ultimately, informal contacts proved to be invaluable in gaining entry. The Center on Work and Family has developed relationships with many corporations in the course of its operations over the last few years. These contacts enabled us to select companies known to be interested in promoting the well-being of low-income families in their communities and then to meet with appropriate company representatives. Interestingly, one company refused to participate because of a pending merger. This company placed all new commitments on hold, whereas a second company, also involved in a merger, saw Project Opportunity as a way of improving morale during a difficult time. Also cited as reasons for not participating were concerns over liability issues of having children in the workplace and union exclusion rules.

Two of the five corporations approached agreed to serve as Project sites. While there was initial enthusiasm for a program that addresses both the needs of some of their employees and the next generation of workers, a great deal of time was spent describing the value of the Project for employers and employees alike and allaying the concerns of worksite personnel and corporate relations departments through meetings and informal discussions. Employees at different levels in the hierarchy need to be committed in different ways and may be persuaded by different arguments. For example, senior corporate executives needed to be convinced of the Project's merit for community relations with minimal disruption in the worksite. Managers were concerned about the allocation of time needed to support the Project, given the demands of their jobs, as well as the effect their involvement might have on other community programs, such as a tutoring program in a nearby high school, to which they were already committed. Some line workers were suspicious of the paternalistic nature of social programs sponsored by institutions in which they had little power or control.

Ultimately, top level executives' commitment was needed to gain access to employees and to provide the support services necessary to conduct the Project. Employees in personnel who were instructed to assist us were most helpful when they, too, were committed to the Project. At each site, Project staff had numerous meetings and telephone conversations with a variety of employees who assisted us by printing address labels, mailing letters, writing announcements for corporate newsletters, and recruiting participants and mentors, among other tasks.

Securing Funding for the Project

From initial conversations with federal agencies, it was clear that to be competitive at the national level, Project Opportunity would need to move beyond the planning phase and (1) develop a detailed intervention protocol, (2) test its feasibility and provide outcome data by running a pilot program, and (3) plan an experimental design with a matched control group and standardized measures with known reliability and validity. Given the developmental stage of the Project, we were encouraged by federal project officers to seek local funding for the initial phases of the Project. Although intrigued by the program, some local foundations were reluctant to fund a demonstration project. They viewed their mission as providing support for ongoing programs that provided direct services to the neediest of Boston's population–those families living in persistent poverty. In addition, they were wary of funding university-based projects because they believed that these institutions were already rich in resources and did little in terms of reaching out to the needs of surrounding low-income communities.

The largest private foundation in Boston, the Boston Foundation, awarded initial funding after an extensive review process that convinced them of the potential of Project Opportunity for demonstrating the benefit of public/private partnerships in addressing the family needs of low-wage employees and the social problems which challenge the neighborhoods in which they reside. In addition, the two businesses selected as program sites contributed substantial financial resources to the Project, in part, because they believed it was a way of improving morale during a time of corporate downsizing and mergers that were occurring at both institutions.

Conducting Focus Groups and a Community Needs Assessment Survey

The next step was to conduct focus groups with potential participants and a needs assessment survey with a larger group at the two worksites in order to ensure that the Project was responsive to the distinctive needs of the program participants. These efforts were also intended to elicit support for the Project from the various constituents. Eight focus groups were conducted across the two worksites: two involved 35 teens recruited from local youth groups, and the remaining six involved working parents, predominantly from low-income Boston neighborhoods who responded to flyers at the worksites because of their desire to learn more about Project Opportunity.

The focus group meetings were audio-recorded, then transcribed, greatly facilitating qualitative analysis (the interview schedule is available on request). The transcriptions were reviewed by three people: a staff member who attended the meetings, a staff member who did not attend, and a graduate student assistant unfamiliar with the Project. This process provided information on the topics specified in the agenda for discussion as well as new themes that emerged during the groups. Primary themes were seen as those that occurred consistently across all three reviewers and are presented below.

Parents spoke of their concerns about raising teens in the city while working full-time. Worried about the drug activity and violence that plagued their neighborhoods, they wanted support and guidance in helping their children remain safe, resist negative peer pressure, and succeed academically. Some parents were afraid that their family concerns were spilling over into the workplace and that their supervisors would be unsympathetic. Parents also provided information about the kinds of incentives which would facilitate program participation, such as babysitting services, transportation for younger participants, and scheduling the family meetings at the end of the work day.

The adolescents in the focus groups were also concerned about problems in their neighborhood and believed that a program like Program Opportunity would provide adolescents with new ideas about how to succeed. Most stated that they would be interested in participating in the Project, citing the career mentorship as an appealing way to learn more about career opportunities. They were also interested in learning about computers and receiving a diploma at the end of the program year. The youth also supported the idea of a family support group; the topic they most wanted to talk about was sexual activity. The teens believed that their parents would not participate in the program given the other demands that affect their families. When it was pointed out to them that services would be provided at the workplace, not the school, they thought that we would be able to recruit more families.

Knowledge gained from the focus groups was used to construct a community needs questionnaire that was administered to a larger sample of families employed by one of the two businesses (the questionnaire is available on request). A total of 250 adolescents and their parents completed the survey for $10 payment and a raffle ticket for $50 gift certificates to a local supermarket chain. The survey was useful in recruiting participants to the Project, and, as analysis proceeds, it will provide additional insights into the target population. Since respondents represent a diverse group in terms of urban vs. suburban residence, racial and ethnic background, and socioeconomic status, the survey will enable comparison of program participants to nonparticipants and of the target population to other families with teens.

Preliminary analyses revealed some interesting findings. Urban teenagers reported hanging out alone and being home alone less frequently than did suburban teenagers. Both urban teenagers and their parents reported more negative attitudes toward their neighborhoods than the suburban respondents, but the complaints they did make were complementary. That is, urban residents reported their neighborhoods were too noisy and congested, while suburban residents complained about feeling isolated from other people. Both sets of respondents reported too few safe places for teens to spend time.

Developing Outcome Measures

Standardized instruments and questions developed specifically for this Project by key constituents will be used in all phases of the data collection. Initial instrument selection involved a careful review of the literature and input from the Project staff. Decisions were based on several criteria, including cultural relevance of the measures, ease of administration, reliability, and validity. While standardized measures of known reliability, validity, and published norms are always preferred, some new measures were designed and some standardized measures were modified to improve relevance for the target population. All measures were pilot tested on parents and adolescents for reliability before finalizing them for the main study.

Examples of the standardized measures that assess the target behaviors defined earlier include a set of self-report questions from the NIDA Monitoring the Future Survey (Johnson, O'Malley, & Bachman, 1993) that asks adolescents about their substance use, perceptions, and attitudes; the Child Behavior Checklist (Achenbach & Edelbrock, 1983) which asks parents to respond to a wide variety of clinical concerns about their children including depression and aggressive behavior; and the Academic Efficacy Scale (Seidman, 1991), a self-report measure to assess school success and failure in teenagers. Measures developed specifically for this Project include assessments of informal social supports, of the ways teens spend their after-school and weekend time, and familiarity of participants with local resources for families.

Since face validity of the measures is important in gaining credibility with non-professional constituents (Bry & George, 1979), comments were solicited from multiple constituents before final decisions were made. Some members of the Steering Committee were concerned that the battery of instruments focused too much on symptomatology and not enough on adaptive coping skills, such as church attendance, equitable gender-role experiences within families, and the importance of family loyalty and extended kinships. The subcommittee to review the measures, described above, allows substantial input from community representatives.

In addition to assessing outcomes on the basis of goals initially defined, the Project should be assessed by the participants themselves in terms of what they hope to gain from their involvement. This requires collecting periodic data on participant expectations for different program components. Participants' assessments of the services received should be part of an outcome evaluation as well. Acknowledging that expectations and opinions can change over time suggests that information should be elicited during the course of the program as well as upon enrollment and at completion.

One technique developed to encourage ongoing, short-term evaluation by the participants themselves uses self-assigned homework generated from the monthly family education meetings. At the end of the discussion, each participant generates a list of specific attitudes or behaviors to modify during the following month, derived from that evening's topic. Part of each subsequent family meeting includes an informal review of the success of these efforts. In addition, the evaluator keeps these lists and self-reports of subsequent compliance, both as outcome measures and as tools to assess the utility of the family meetings in addressing the participants' concerns.

PHASE THREE: IMPLEMENTING THE PILOT PROGRAM

In order to refine the logistics of the program, and demonstrate its feasibility to funders and constituents alike, pilot groups were initiated at each worksite, consisting of nine to eleven adolescents and a parent of each. In this section, we will present the steps taken to recruit and retain participants in the Project, to build a commitment on the part of the participants and staff to the data collection, and to conduct a process evaluation.

Recruiting and Retaining the Participants

Participant Recruitment

Families were recruited with the active support and partnership of workplace personnel assigned to the Project, who were often personally committed to the program. These employees gave legitimacy to the Project, helped recruit mentors, and provided introductions to potential participants. Additional recruitment strategies included placing notices in strategic locations at the worksites, advertisements in the company newsletters, and occasionally sitting at a table outside the company cafeteria for two hours during lunch periods to hand out flyers and try to sell the program to passersby. Families were accepted on a first-come, first-served basis.

Participants in the pilot groups constituted a racially diverse group: about half were African-American, with the remainder divided between white and Latino. All were full-time employees, working 40 hours per week, primarily as secretaries. Married women reported that their husbands worked full-time as well. The median number of children was two, and household composition varied from one parent with two children, to two parents with four children and one granddaughter. The participating families lived in the surrounding low-income neighborhoods of the two worksites.

While it was anticipated that the families in the pilot study would fit the defined target population but might be those least in need of services, initial data collection revealed that the participants indeed reflected the strengths and vulnerabilities anticipated in the target population. To date, the participants have been primarily mothers, with only two fathers ever attending, while adolescent boys and girls were equally represented. Efforts are being made to encourage fathers of currently participating families to accompany their children to the family support and education meetings. A subcommittee of the Steering Committee is being formed to address ways of attracting men.

Participant Retention

In order to ensure participant retention, a number of techniques have been implemented to create a sense of belonging, including periodic appreciation activities, such as a mid-year social event, the distribution of Project Opportunity T-shirts, and ongoing support from the Project staff. As a result of suggestions made by adolescents who participated in the focus groups, a $500 stipend will be awarded to each adolescent who successfully completes the program. In order to make attendance more convenient for participants, a simple dinner is served at the family support and education meetings, babysitting is offered, meetings are held at the parents' worksite at the end of a workday on a day of the week chosen by the participants, and efforts have been made to provide transportation for some adolescents.

Given the demands of urban, low-income families, participants may experience a variety of concerns, such as school difficulties, health concerns, and legal conflicts. The Project Coordinator maintains ongoing contact with participants, serving as a source of support, facilitating referrals to appropriate agencies and providing advocacy services when necessary. In the future, graduates of the program will be invited to play a substantial role in the orientation process and as a potential resource for recruiting and retaining new participants.

Building the Commitment of the Participants and Staff to the Evaluation

Incentive structures are needed not only to encourage participants to comply with the evaluation process, but also to ensure that staff support this aspect of the program (Torres, 1991; Weiss, 1987). Often staff involved in service delivery have little research training and may feel that the rigor of a formal evaluation interferes with program implementation (Small, 1990a). Their confidence in the credibility of the measures is essential for the timely and thorough collection of the data. Alternatively, their lack of endorsement of the data collection will undermine its value for the program participants and further impede data collection.

The Project evaluator found that eliciting feedback from the staff at every step of the process on the timing, content, wording, and presentation of the evaluation measures was helpful in increasing compliance by staff, since they felt more involved in this aspect of the Project. In addition, the ongoing availability of the evaluator to remind Project staff to complete evaluation forms, provide quick responses to questions, and to point out the relevance of a strong evaluation process to their work encourages compliance (Small, 1990a,b).

Incentives are also necessary to promote compliance of participants in an outcome evaluation, hence several techniques were planned, including attendance of the Project evaluator at the initial family meetings and completion of a contract/consent form describing the self-reports as a responsibility of participants. Indeed, some parents saw their provision of self-report data as repayment for receipt of free services. Ongoing discussions of the confidentiality of the data were important. Some parents were concerned that this information could be given to employers. Identification numbers, rather than names, were used on the questionnaires so that only the Project evaluator could match surveys to individuals. Corporate personnel had been advised and understood that they would not have access to the data. Although the confidentiality measures had been explained to participants at the onset of the pilot Project, repeated assurances were necessary.

Some parents were reluctant to respond to questions about socially undesirable behavior such as substance abuse and sexual activity. Subsequent discussions with parents and the Steering Committee revealed that prior negative experiences may have contributed to their fears that the data could be misinterpreted and perpetuate stereotypes about race and urban adolescents. Assuring participants that the questions were from standardized measures given to participants regardless of their race and socioeconomic status was less helpful in allaying their fears than was raising these issues with them and listening to their concerns.

Observation of selected family meetings facilitated data collection by providing information that could not be obtained in any other way. For example, obstacles to the collection of time-consuming survey data from the participants became apparent: some parents were wary of providing personal data such as age and income. Providing time for the self-reports during the family support and education meetings, administering them over two meetings, and waiting until participants were more engaged in the programs before administering the most sensitive measures facilitated completion in a timely manner, with a 100% response rate and little missing data.

Conducting a Process Evaluation

A process evaluation is crucial to a successful program for two reasons: (1) to provide "rapid feedback" for "midcourse correction" of an ongoing program, and (2) to facilitate replication of a successful program (McGraw, McKinlay, & McClements et al., 1989). Our efforts to accomplish both of these tasks will be presented below.

Providing Ongoing Feedback to Project Staff

In order to meet the goal of providing rapid feedback to the program, several techniques were implemented. Each survey requested open-ended comments from the participants about the program operation. Weekly to monthly individual contact with the Project Coordinator further encouraged comments in a more casual setting. To date, participants have been more willing to express their positive and negative feelings in conversations with the Project Coordinator. Biweekly staff meetings have provided an opportunity for open discussion of emerging issues, with suggestions incorporated into future program activities. While these formal meetings have succeeded in eliciting staff feedback, sharing office space, and hence engaging in frequent informal contact among the evaluator and other Project staff, continues to be an invaluable source of information.

Providing Information for Program Replication

In order to meet the process evaluation goal of replicating the program, several key questions must be addressed, as suggested by McGraw, McKinlay, McClements et al. (1989). Is the impact of the program consistent across families? Does the program vary in implementation by site? In order to assess the program impact on each family, extensive records are necessary to determine the extent of actual participation in the program components. Telephone and in-person contacts with each family must be recorded to ascertain how important they are for participant retention and for desired outcomes. Those staff members who are collecting these data have been involved in designing the specific techniques and forms to be used in order to ensure their practical utility and to increase the likelihood they will be carefully implemented. Ongoing revision of these systems is anticipated. These records, in conjunction with evaluator observation of program activities, will allow a comparison to be made by program site. Records of paid and volunteer time and other costs of each program activity will clearly aid program replication.

Analysis of the effects of various program components will be supplemented by asking the participants and other constituents which components they thought were most important and why. While parents were clearly attracted to the Project for its mentoring component, feedback suggests that the family group meetings have provided them with useful information in terms of parenting strategies. The adolescents think the family meetings are fun, in part, because the curriculum has included a number of experiential exercises. Besides providing data, asking participants for feedback promotes goodwill and feelings of mutual respect with Project staff.

PHASE FOUR: EXPANDING THE PROGRAM

Project Opportunity began full implementation in 1997 for three years. A total of 100-150 adolescents and their parents will participate in the program, in cohorts of ten at various worksites. Entrance into the program is being staggered over the first year in order to ensure that corrective feedback from the ongoing process evaluation can be applied to succeeding groups.

Identifying Additional Project Sites

New worksites are now being sought to add diversity to the program participants, to provide a larger pool of potential participants, and to increase the Project's visibility in the community. This will include smaller, community-based companies, such as insurance companies, limousine services, and independent telecommunications companies. These businesses are being recruited through the local chambers of commerce within these communities. Family support and education groups will be offered either at one of these workplaces or within local community centers.

Recruiting a Comparison Group

While the use of an experimental design with random assignment to experimental groups is an ideal goal, its utility for evaluation of programs operating in natural settings is questionable (Terborg, 1988). Random selection and random assignment to control and treatment groups are unlikely to be feasible for a program requiring active participation such as Project Opportunity. As Terborg argues, "inconsistency of results" may not be due to insufficient methodological rigor, but rather to the complexity of the social context within which programs are implemented. In the absence of a true experimental design, a matched comparison group could, however, lend validity to the evaluation.

Our plan beyond the pilot phase of the project is to include a comparison group. Subjects will be recruited primarily through families interested in participating but unable to do so for logistical reasons. Incentives for their participation in data collection have been discussed with various constituents. It was agreed that enrollment in a lottery for a family trip to a resort such as Disney World might be a more successful recruitment technique than paying each family a modest amount for their time. Comparison subjects will be interviewed three times: first, to collect parental and adolescent background data, including the outcome measures described above; second, at one year; and, third, at two years, to repeat the outcome measures. Matching will be based on adolescents' age, gender, and other cultural characteristics such as race, ethnicity, and social class.

Securing Additional Funding Resources

In addition to pursuing additional funding for the expansion phase of the Project at the national level, we continue to seek local money to complete the pilot phase. Towards that end, our two major funders, The Bank of Boston and The Boston Foundation brought together local corporations and foundations at a breakfast to present Project Opportunity. Many of those attending have expressed an interest in Project Opportunity, and we are in the process of discussing with them the possibility of funding from their Boards. The community relations offices of our present business sites are in the process of arranging for media coverage to increase the visibility of the Project.

CONCLUSION

The process of developing a program such as Project Opportunity has been shown to be a long-term effort, spanning several years to reach the pilot implementation phase of operations. This prolonged time span is in part due to the choice of a comprehensive community-wide partnership model among researchers, practitioners, funders, workplace personnel, community leaders, mentors and the participants in all phases of the design, implementation, and evaluation of the Project. Broad inclusion of Project constituents was enhanced by several techniques: the establishment of a Steering Committee, using focus groups and a needs assessment survey to hear from the target population, and ongoing formal and informal discussions between Project staff and other constituents to elicit advice and to clarify our goals.

We encourage other programs to utilize this approach and to report their successes and failures within the professional community. The lessons learned from this Project could be helpful in developing prevention programs for other special populations such as homeless women at greater risk for substance abuse, physical and sexual assault, and depression (Buckner, Bassuk, & Zima, 1993; D'Ercole & Struening, 1990), and gay and lesbian teens at greater risk for suicide and threats of violence (Morrow, 1993; Rotheram-Borus, Hunter, & Rosario, 1994).

REFERENCES

Achenbach, T., & Edelbrock, C. (1983). *Manual for the Child Behavior Checklist and Revised Child Behavior Profile.* Burlington, VT: University of Vermont.

Barone, C., Weissberg, R., Kasprow, W., Voyce, C., Arthur, M., & Shriver, T. (1995). Involvement in multiple problem behaviors of young urban adolescents. *The Journal of Primary Prevention, 15*(3), 261-283.

Bry, B., & George, R. (1979). Evaluating and improving prevention programs: A strategy from drug abuse. *Evaluation and Program Planning, 2*, 127-136.

Buckner, J., Bassuk, E., & Zima, B. (1993). Mental health issues affecting homeless women: Implications for intervention. *American Journal of Orthopsychiatry, 63* (3), 385-399.

Calabrese, R., & Schumer, H. (1986). The effects of service activities on adolescent alienation. *Adolescence, 21*: 675-687.

Caplan, M., & Weissberg, R. (1989). Promoting social competence in early adolescence: Developmental considerations. In B. H. Schneider, G. Attili, J. Nadel, & R. Weissberg (Eds.), *Social competence in developmental perspective* (pp. 371-385). Boston, MA: Kluwer.

Carnegie Foundation (1992). *A matter of time: Risks and opportunity in the non-school hours.* Woodlawn, MD: Wolk Press, Inc.

Colan, N., Mague, K., Cohen, R., & Schneider, R. (1994). Family education in the workplace: A prevention program for working parents and school-age children. *Journal of Primary Prevention, 15*: 161-172.

Compas, B., Hinden, B., & Gerhardt, C. (1995). Adolescent development: Pathways and processes of risk and resilience. *Annual Review of Psychology, 46*, 265-293.

D'Ercole, A., & Struening, E. (1990). Victimization among homeless women: Implications for service delivery. *Journal of Community Psychology, 18* (2), 141-152.

Dryfoos, J. (1990). *Adolescents at risk: Prevalence and prevention.* New York: Oxford University Press.

Feldman, S., & Elliot, G. (Eds.) (1990). *At the threshold: The developing adolescent.* Cambridge, MA: Harvard University Press.

Felner, R., Brand, S., Mulhall, K., Counter, B., Millman, J., & Fried, J. (1994). The parenting partnership: The evaluation of a human service/corporate workplace collaboration for the prevention of substance abuse and mental health problems, and the promotion of family and work adjustment. *The Journal of Primary Prevention, 15,* 123-146.

Funkhauser, J. (1993). Programs and tools to build resiliency. *The Prevention Pipeline.* Rockville, MD: National Clearinghouse for Alcohol and Drug Information, Substance Abuse and Mental Health Services Administration.

Garbarino, J., Dubrow, N., Kostelny, K., & Pardo, C. (1992). *Children in danger.* San Francisco, CA: Jossey-Bass Publishers.

Garmezy, N. (1993). Children in poverty: Resilience despite risk. *Psychiatry, 56,* 127-136.

Gibbs, J. (1988). *Young, black and male in America: An endangered species.* Dover, MA: Auburn House.

Googins, B., Hudson, R., & Pitt-Catsouphes, M. (1995). Strategic responses: Corporate involvement in family and community issues. *Work-Family Policy Paper series.* Boston, MA: Center on Work and Family.

Haggerty, R., Sherrod, L., Garmezy, N., & Rutter, M. (1994). *Stress, risk, and resilience in children and adolescents: Processes, mechanisms, and interventions.* Cambridge, MA: Cambridge University Press.

Hamilton, S. (1990). *Apprenticeship for adulthood.* New York: The Free Press.

Hamilton, S., & Fenzel, L. (1988). The impact of volunteer experience on adolescent social development: Evidence of program effects. *Journal of Adolescent Research, 3*: 65-80.

Hauser, S., & Bowlds, M. (1990). Stress, coping and adaptation. In S. Feldman & G. Elliot (Eds.), *At the threshold: The developing adolescent.* Cambridge, MA: Harvard University Press.

Hess, P., & Mullen, E. (Ed.) (1995). *Practitioner-researcher partnership: Building knowledge from, in, and for practice.* Washington, DC: NASW Press.

Jacobs, F. (1988). The five-tiered approach to evaluation: Context and implementation. In H. Weiss & F. Jacobs (Eds.), *Evaluating family programs* (pp. 37-68). New York: Aldine de Gruyter.

Jessor, R. (1993). Successful adolescent development among youth in high-risk settings. *American Psychologist, 48,* 117-126.

Jobs for the Future (1993). *Creating an American style youth apprenticeship program: A formative evaluation of Project Pro-tech.* Cambridge: MA: Jobs for the Future.

Johnson, L., O'Malley, P., & Bachman, J. (1993). *National survey results on drug use from Monitoring the Future Study, 1975-1992.* Rockville, MD: National Institute on Drug Abuse, NIH Publication No. 93-3597.

Kazdin, A. (1993). Adolescent mental health: Prevention and treatment programs. *American Psychologist, 48*(2), 127-141.

Luthar, S. (1993). Annotation: Methodological and conceptual issues in research on childhood resilience. *Journal of Child Psychology and Psychiatry, 34*(4), 441-453.

McGraw, S., McKinlay, S., McClements, L., Lasater, T., Assaf, A., & Carelton, R. (1989). Methods in program evaluation: The process evaluation system of the Pawtucket Heart Health Program. *Evaluation Review, 13*(5), 459-483.

Morrow, D. (1993). Social work with gay and lesbian adolescents. *Social Work, 38* (6), 655- 660.

National Research Council (1993). *Losing generations.* Washington, DC: National Academy Press.

Nelson, T. (1989). Involving families in substance abuse prevention. *Family Relations, 38*, 306-310.

Prothrow-Stith, D. (1991). *Deadly consequences.* New York: Harper Collins Publishers.

Richters, J., & Martinez, P. (1993). The NIMH community violence project: I. Children as victims of and witnesses to violence. *Psychiatry, 56*, 7-21.

Rotheram-Borus, M., Hunter, J., & Rosario, M. (1994). Suicidal behavior and gay-related stress among gay and bisexual male adolescents. *Journal of Adolescent Research, 9,* 498-508.

Safyer, A. (1994). The impact of inner-city life on adolescent development: Implications for practice. *Smith College of Social Work Studies, 64*, 153-167.

Safyer, A., Litchfield, L., & Leahy, B. (1996). Employees with teens: The role of EAP needs assessments. *Employee Assistance Quarterly, 11*, 47-66.

Safyer, A., Velez, L., & Colan, N. (1994). *Engaging urban families through their workplaces: An innovative prevention strategy.* Paper presented at National Association of Social Workers Annual Conference, Nashville, TN.

Schinke, S. P., & Gilcrest, L. D. (1985). Preventing substance abuse with children and adolescents. *Journal of Consulting and Clinical Psychology, 53,* 596-602.

Seidman, E. (1991). Growing up the hard way: Pathways of urban adolescents. *American Journal of Community Psychology, 19*, 173-205.

Small, S. (1990a). *Preventive programs that support families with adolescents.* Working paper. Washington, DC: Carnegie Council on Adolescent Development.

Small, S. (1990b). Some issues regarding the evaluation of family life education programs. *Family Relations, 39*, 132-135.

Spencer, M. B., & Dornbusch, S. (1990). Challenges in studying minority youth. In S. Feldman & G. Elliot (Eds.), *At the threshold: The developing adolescent.* Cambridge, MA: Harvard University Press.

Terbog, J. (1988). Organizational context. In K. Johnson, J. LaRosa, C. J. Scheirer, & J. Wolle (Eds.), *Proceedings of the 1988 methodological issues in worksite research workshop* (pp. 21-40). Washington, DC: U.S. Department of Health and Human Services, National Institutes of Health.

Torres, R. (1991). Improving the quality of internal evaluation: The evaluator as consultant-mediator. *Evaluation and Program Planning, 14*, 189-198.

Weiss, C. H. (1987). Evaluating social programs: What have we learned? *Society*, *25*(I), 40-45.

Weiss, H., & Jacobs, F. (Eds.) (1988). *Evaluating family programs.* New York, NY: Aldine de Gruyter.

Weissberg, R., Caplan, M., & Harwood, R. (1991). Promoting competent young people in competence-enhancing environments: A systems-based perspective on primary prevention. *Journal of Consulting and Clinical Psychology, 59*(6), 830-841.

West, S., Aiken, L., & Todd, M. (1993). Probing the effects of individual components in multiple component prevention programs. *American Journal of Community Psychology, 21*(5), 571-578.

Wilson-Brewer, R., Cohen, S., O'Donnell, L., & Goodman, I. (1991). *Violence prevention for young adolescents: A survey of the state of the art.* A working paper. Washington, DC: Carnegie Council on Adolescent Development.

Methodological Issues
in Social Work Research
with Depressed Women of Color

Debora M. Ortega
Cheryl A. Richey

EDITORS' NOTE. This article presents a detailed description of conceptual, methodological, and measurement issues pertaining to research with ethnic minority women. The following generalizable research principles and suggestions for future research emerge from this work: (1) While it has long been recognized that most measurement instruments are ethnocentric and gender-biased in relation to constructs of cognition such as intelligence, there has been somewhat less awareness of this in relation to constructs of affect such as depression. Researchers need to recognize that emotions may be social constructions and are likely to be experienced and expressed differently by members of diverse cultures. Therefore, extensive work is needed in appropriate scale construction using the methods described (for example, comparison of factor structures across different populations; establishment of various forms of metric equivalence; and creative scaling such as visual analog scales). (2) The influence of demand characteristics such as social desirability is manifested differently by members of different cultures, and traditional strategies to correct these biases pose additional problems in

---

Debora M. Ortega and Cheryl A. Richey are affiliated with the School of Social Work, University of Washington, Seattle, WA.

Address correspondence to Cheryl A. Richey, School of Social Work, University of Washington (Box 354900), 4101 15th Avenue, N.E., Seattle, WA 98105-6299.

[Haworth co-indexing entry note]: "Methodological Issues in Social Work Research with Depressed Women of Color." Ortega, Debora M., and Cheryl A. Richey. Co-published simultaneously in *Journal of Social Service Research* (The Haworth Press, Inc.) Vol. 23, No. 3/4, 1998, pp. 47-70; and: *Social Work Research with Minority and Oppressed Populations: Methodological Issues and Innovations* (ed: Miriam Potocky, and Antoinette Y. Rodgers-Farmer) The Haworth Press, Inc., 1998, pp. 47-70. Single or multiple copies of this article are available for a fee from The Haworth Document Delivery Service [1-800-342-9678, 9:00 a.m. - 5:00 p.m. (EST). E-mail address: getinfo@haworth.com].

cross-cultural contexts. Therefore, researchers need to have intimate knowledge of cultural norms and values in order to be able to anticipate and account for their influences on responses. As noted by the authors, bicultural/bilingual consultants are indispensable for these reasons. Further, social desirability scales that are culture-specific need to be developed. (3) Methodological diversity and triangulation, while desirable in all research, are particularly important in cross-cultural contexts. (4) It is no longer sufficient to examine gross ethnic group differences (e.g., Hispanics vs. African-Americans vs. Caucasians), or even finer within-group differences (e.g., Mexicans vs. Puerto Ricans, or urban vs. rural African-Americans). Rather, level of acculturation is a crucial factor that needs to be systematically included as an independent variable in all studies involving minority groups. (5) Assessment needs to be expanded to include environmental factors which impact emotional states both positively and negatively. As noted by the authors, the Person-in-Environment system is one available holistic assessment tool that needs to be evaluated in future research. Additional valid and reliable instruments also need to be developed. (6) The oft-cited caveats in the cross-cultural literature regarding issues of entry and rapport-building continue to be valuable recommendations. (7) More research is needed to investigate whether matching of data collectors and respondents on variables such as gender and ethnicity enhances the validity of participants' responses. (8) Finally, the authors note the importance of researcher self-assessment of cross-cultural competence, and suggest relevant techniques in this regard.

SUMMARY. Social work researchers committed to advancing knowledge for effective practice with depressed women, especially culturally-diverse women, are faced with numerous methodological challenges. These challenges emanate from the ambiguity that surrounds the definition and measurement of the concept of depression, and from problems that apply to all cross-cultural research including content, semantic, and technical equivalence of self-report instruments. The article reviews these challenges and concludes with recommendations for addressing them, including suggestions for promoting methodological diversity, cross-cultural measurement validity, consideration of environmental risk and resiliency factors, attention to the process of data collection, and researcher self-assessment. *[Article copies available for a fee from The Haworth Document Delivery Service: 1-800-342-9678. E-mail address: getinfo@haworth.com]*

Depression is considered the leading mental health problem in the United States, affecting more than 8.6 million people (Runck, 1986).

Some would say depression has reached epidemic proportions (Goleman, 1992). Despite the high (and increasing) rate of depression in the American population, the National Institute of Mental Health has recognized that depression is largely underestimated by mental health professionals and the general public (Wetzel, 1978, 1994). Ongoing concerns about detecting and treating depression inspired the National Institute of Mental Health to launch its first major educational campaign in its 40-year history (Runck, 1986).

Research suggests that characteristics of the population most "at risk" for depression include: inadequate education, economic disadvantage, unemployment, low occupational status, and single parenthood with low income (Wetzel, 1984). Women are overrepresented in each of these categories. Consequently, it comes as no surprise that studies of depressive disorder in Western industrial societies, including the United States, repeatedly report significantly higher rates of depression among women than men (e.g., Howell & Bayes, 1981; Jambunathan, 1992; Jenkins, Kleinman, & Good, 1991; Kizilay, 1992; Kleinman & Good, 1985a; Sheppard, 1994; Wetzel, 1994).

Social work researchers and practitioners who are committed to advancing knowledge for effective practice with depressed women, especially culturally-diverse women, are faced with numerous methodological challenges, including those related to assessment and measurement activities. These challenges emanate from two sources: (1) the ambiguity that currently surrounds the definition and operationalization of the concept of depression in the Western or North American literature; and (2) the ever-present task of addressing and minimizing the ethno-cultural bounds inherent in most of the procedures and instruments available for assessing/monitoring client functioning and measuring intervention/program outcomes. This paper will critically review several significant challenges from these two sources and offer guidelines for developing practice research methods, particularly assessment and measurement procedures, which may be more culturally valid and meaningful for women of color who experience different forms of suffering in stressful or unsustaining environmental circumstances. Improving methods for accurately detecting and assessing problematic levels of dysphoria or depression among culturally different individuals is important in order to: (1) reduce instances of false negative diagnosis or failure to detect and treat a valid or serious problem; (2) avoid mislabeling a problem situation and subsequently applying inappropriate/ ineffective interventions, in other words, to ensure a better fit among clients-goals-interventions; (3) expand opportunities for earlier intervention or prevention strategies; (4) enhance engagement and retention of clients of color in social and mental health service agencies; and (5) ensure more culturally-diverse samples in social work practice research.

The article begins by exploring in more detail the two broad methodological challenges faced by social work researchers interested in working with depressed women of color. First, the diffuse construct of "depression" will be examined including the absence of concurrence among researchers about the definition of depression, and the specific characteristics or "factors" of depression as measured by a widely used standardized rating scale. Second, several generic challenges to cross-cultural research will be discussed as these pertain to assessing depression among women of color. For example, issues of cross-cultural validity or "equivalence" in measurement instruments will be considered, including item or content equivalence, and semantic or meaning equivalence. The article concludes with recommendations for addressing these challenges, including enhancing conceptual equivalence of self-report measures, expanding assessment to include consideration of environmental risk and resiliency factors, striving for multiple-method and multiple-source information, and attending to the interpersonal process and context of assessment activities.

DEFINING AND MEASURING "DEPRESSION"

Definitions. A primary methodological challenge in conducting research with depressed women of color, including American women who represent diverse ethnic and cultural backgrounds, is the apparent lack of agreement across studies about what constitutes "depression." Conceptual and empirical articles addressing depression are often unclear about the specific nature of the construct. The definition of depression in the literature spans a relatively large range of features from intra-psychic mood or emotion (dysphoria), to major depressive disorder or illness that includes sustained patterns of somatization and vegetative complaints. For example, a review of published literature on ethnic minority women and depression provided 12 citations; 9 of these articles focused on women and 3 reported investigations of gender differences within and across cultures (Barbee, 1992, 1994; Callahan & Wolinsky, 1994; Canino et al., 1987; Franks & Faux, 1990; Guarnaccia, Angel, & Worobey, 1989; Markides & Farrell, 1985; Napholz, 1994; Shin, 1994; Stroup-Benham, Lawrence, & Trevino, 1989; Vega, Kolody, & Valle, 1986; Warren, 1994). Only one-third of these articles (4 out of 12) articulated a definition of depression. For instance, both Barbee (1994) and Warren (1994) defined depressive symptomatology as dysphoria, sadness, grief, despair or mood disturbance. Barbee's (1994) clearly articulated definition of depression was also empirically supported by qualitative data collected from 15 African-American women. In the other 2 studies, depression was defined simply as a psychiatric disorder, with little attention given to operationalizing it (Kizilay, 1992; Canino et al., 1987). The remaining 8 articles, out of those reviewed, did not specifically define depression.

This brief summary of recent literature focusing on depression among culturally-diverse populations reveals that it is not uncommon for researchers to study "depression" without specifically defining what it is. The vagueness of the depression construct occurs across studies, including those that focus on women and populations of color as well as on more mainstream Caucasian samples. This ubiquitous lack of specificity suggests that many researchers assume that there is general understanding of and agreement with the definition of depression. This assumption is problematic because it ignores the ever-present possibility that depression is uniquely experienced and expressed in different cultural contexts. These differences have important implications for measuring depression in clinical and general populations.

Measurement. The absence of concurrence about the specific components or characteristics of depression has direct implications for assessment and measurement activities. For instance, when the construct of depression is too loosely defined, or too inclusive, confidence in the psychometric properties of available assessment tools used to detect and measure depression is compromised. The specificity of the definition of depression influences an instrument's capacity to detect depression as opposed to other phenomena such as anxiety (Breslau, 1987).

Despite uneven attention to operationalization, the nature of the construct of depression can be inferred to some degree from the measurement instruments selected for use in studies with community or psychiatric samples. For instance, 4 of the 12 studies reviewed employed the CES-D (Center for Epidemiologic Studies Depression scale), and one study utilized the DIS (Diagnostic Interview Schedule) as the primary measure of depression.

Concerns about measurement validity have been raised by depression researchers in relation to several widely-used instruments, including the CES-D. The CES-D will be discussed in more detail here because it is frequently selected for use in larger-sample community studies of depression.

The reliability and validity of the CES-D have been determined for the general population through factor analysis. For example, Radloff (1977) was the first to report the presence of a theoretically-determined four factor structure utilizing the CES-D with a primarily "White" population of 4996 community and 70 psychiatric inpatient respondents. The four factors include:

1. *Depressed Affect.* This factor reflects feelings or expressions of sadness and isolation, and includes such items as "had the blues," "felt depressed," "had crying spells," "felt lonely."
2. *Positive Affect.* This factor reflects contentment with or enjoyment of life, and includes: "felt good," "hopeful," "happy," "enjoyed life." These items are reverse coded to indicate a deficiency of positive feelings.
3. *Somatic Symptoms.* This factor contains items relating to physical difficulties or lack of energy, for example, "felt bothered," "poor appetite," "everything was an effort," "sleep was restless," "couldn't get going."
4. *Interpersonal Distress.* This factor assesses respondents' interpretation of other people's behavior toward them, specifically whether others are unfriendly toward or dislike them.

Four items on the CES-D did not load on any of the four factors at or above the standard .40 level in Radloff's study. These items were: "you thought your life had been a failure," "you had trouble keeping your mind on what you were doing," "you felt fearful," and "you talked less than usual."

Studies have continued to utilize factor analysis in determining the applicability of the CES-D to other populations since Radloff (1977) first identified the four factor structure. These studies have utilized two approaches–confirmatory and exploratory factor analysis. The first approach, confirmatory factor analysis, is often used when comparing the applicability of the CES-D in ethnic minority populations. When this method is employed, the four factor structure reported by Radloff emerges despite language and cultural differences (Roberts, Rhoades, & Vernon, 1990; Roberts, Vernon, & Rhoades, 1989). For example, Roberts and colleagues (1989, 1990) report in their study of Mexican Americans, over 68% of whom were men, that their target factors were adapted from Radloff's previous factor analysis of CES-D scores in which a four factor solution appeared to adequately represent the data. Thus, the factors utilized by Roberts and colleagues were preconstructed. This means that the experiences of depression as reported by people representing the more dominant or mainstream segments of American society were used as the framework or structure to measure depression in a sample that included ethnic minorities.

Exploratory factor analysis is the second approach that has been employed to understand the validity of the CES-D in culturally-different populations (Callahan & Wolinsky, 1994; Guarnaccia, Angel, & Worobey, 1989; Stroup-Benham, Lawrence, & Trevino, 1989). These researchers advocate the use of exploratory factor analysis in determining the fit between the CES-D as a measure of depression with ethnic minority populations because this strategy allows for other factor structures to emerge that may better represent the data, and consequently promotes the development of more culturally-grounded (and gender-relevant) theories of depression.

Exploratory factor analytic studies of the CES-D with ethnically-diverse populations often report at least some variation in item distribution across the standard four factors, if not more pronounced differences in the basic factor structure. For example, while Callahan and Wolinsky (1994) found a four factor structure among African-American elderly females that was similar in many ways to Radloff's analysis, others have found that the CES-D items presented a different factor structure with Hispanic populations (Guarnaccia et al., 1989; Stroup-Benham et al., 1989). For illustration, the findings from these latter two studies will be discussed in more detail.

Guarnaccia and colleagues (1989) utilized the Hispanic Health and Nutrition Examination Survey (HHANES) data to compare rates of depression across three Hispanic populations: Mexican Americans, Puerto Ricans, and Cubans. The data were analyzed across ethnicity, gender and language. The data indicated differences in depression across the three ethnic groups and across gender within each group. The results also showed differences in gender and language (English versus Spanish) for Puerto Rican and Mexican Americans. Language preference was indicated by respondents' choice of English or Spanish for the interview. Cuban Americans were eliminated from this analysis because of the low number of English-speaking respondents. Hispanic women experienced different factor structures than their male counterparts.

This study reported that the factor structures among Cuban, Puerto Rican and Mexican American women were relatively similar to each other, and different from patterns found among the Hispanic men. For example, while Mexican American men approximated the "White" factor structure proposed by Radloff, the Mexican American women combined items from Radloff's factors of depressed affect, somatic symptoms, and positive affect. Twelve items combined for the first factor: "bothered," "had the blues," "couldn't keep mind on things," "depressed," "everything an effort," "failure," "fearful," "restless sleep," "happy," "lonely," "crying," and "sad." The second factor drew from interpersonal items such as "unfriendly" and "disliked." The third factor comprised positive affect and included "good," "hopeful," "happy," and "enjoyed life."

Puerto Rican women also combined the affective and somatic items from the scale as a first factor. In addition to the items reported by the Mexican American female respondents, four additional items loaded for the Puerto Rican women. These items were "poor appetite," "enjoyed life," "talked less," and "couldn't get going." The second factor, interpersonal, was identical to the Mexican American women. The third factor included only "good" and "hopeful."

The factor structure for the Cuban women was slightly different from both Mexican American and Puerto Rican women. For instance, Cuban women had a lower number of items in the first factor. The authors proposed that this factor represents isolation rather than a combination of affective and somatic symptoms (Guarnaccia et al., 1989) . The first factor, isolation, is comprised of the items: "failure," "lonely," "unfriendly," "crying," "sad," "disliked," and "couldn't get going." The second factor, depressed affect, is comprised of "bothered by things," "trouble keeping your mind on what you were doing," and "talked less." The final factor, positive affect, was identical to the Puerto Rican sample and included "felt good" and "hopeful."

Stroup-Benham and associates (1989) utilized the same data from the HHANES study to investigate differences in depression among women with children who were members of single-parent and coupled families. The study focused on Puerto Rican and Mexican American women and employed exploratory factor analysis to investigate depression. The factor loadings of the CES-D in this study varied according to ethnicity and marital status, and for the most part, did not reflect the results reported by other researchers (e.g., Guarnaccia et al., 1989; Radloff, 1977; Roberts, 1983, 1989, 1990). A subgroup of Mexican American coupled females in this study (Stroup-Benham et al., 1989) were the only respondents who came close to matching the loadings reported by Guarnaccia and colleagues (1989). The factor loadings of all the other subgroups varied, and included the shifting of several items between factors, and the reorganization of items into three, four, and five factor structures. Further, these factor groups did not always correspond with current theoretical tenets of depression for Hispanic or ethnic-minority female populations (Stroup-Benham et al., 1989). These data suggest caution when utilizing the CES-D across Mexican American or Cuban households because of differences not only across but within the various Hispanic groups, depending on marital/living status (single versus coupled).

Despite differences between studies, overall factor analytic research with Hispanic women, using the CES-D, has found a first factor combining depressed affect and somatic symptoms (Guarnaccia et al., 1989; Stroup-Benham et al., 1989). These findings are in basic accord with several cross-cultural theories of depression that indicate that some ethnic minority groups experience depression or express interpersonal and personal distress or dysphoric affect through somatization more so than the general population (Beiser, 1985; Chang, 1985; Guarnaccia et al., 1989; Schwartz & Schwartz, 1993; Song, 1991; Stroup-Benham et al., 1989; Tabora & Flaskerud, 1994). Thus, when compared with middle-class Caucasian Americans who may be more likely to express depression as an intra-psychic or psychological phenomenon, some ethnic populations communicate sadness, hopelessness, or demoralization more as bodily complaints, which may serve as a metaphor for suffering. For example, in addition to the findings reported for Hispanic women, other research suggests that Chinese Americans may somatize depressive symptoms more frequently than do dominant culture clients (Tabora & Flaskerud, 1994), and that Laotian Hmong adolescent refugees in the U.S. often use terms for various states of "difficult liver" (nyuai siab) to convey the concept of depression (Dunnigan, McNall, & Mortimer, 1993).

Interestingly, although the CES-D includes items that tap the somatic dimension of depression, these are relatively few when compared to the number of other items reflecting more psycho-emotional symptoms. This observation suggests that the psychometric properties of the CES-D, and perhaps other standard measures that have been normed on mainstream populations, may underestimate the range and magnitude of depressive symptoms if these are experienced and expressed by people from different cultural backgrounds as largely "sociosomatic" phenomena (e.g., Kleinman & Good, 1985b). The term "sociosomatic" reflects the position taken by a number of anthropologists and cross-cultural psychologists who argue that emotional states are largely culturally constructed and represent an integration of bodily experiences and communication in particular sociocultural contexts (Jenkins, Kleinman, & Good, 1991).

The next section reviews several fundamental challenges that apply to all cross-cultural research. Specifically, questions related to measurement equivalence or cross-cultural validity will be addressed as these relate to research on depression.

CROSS-CULTURAL VALIDITY

The methodological challenges presented by the definitions of and attempts to measure depression as discussed previously are further compounded by the additional complexities of assessing depression across individuals and groups that represent diverse cultural, racial, or ethnic backgrounds. Expressions of depressive states or suffering–the language of emotion–can vary considerably within and across groups of people that reflect different cultural affiliations (Jenkins, Kleinman, & Good, 1991). These variations, even within subgroup populations, require special attention and consideration if social work researchers are to avoid distortions of meaning, biased interpretations, and overlooking what is culturally particular with clients and research participants.

Despite their notable limitations, standard self-report instruments, like the CES-D, remain the main channel through which most research participants, including ethnic minority respondents, communicate to social scientists their "languages of emotion"–their experiences and feelings of dysphoria, demoralization, and hopelessness. For example, a review of 80 American research studies of multicultural counseling and intervention outcomes with racial/ethnic minorities reported that a large majority of these studies utilized traditional paper-and-pencil tests developed for middle-class Caucasian groups as the major or only treatment outcome measure (Ponterotto & Casas, 1991). In light of this finding, it is not surprising that most critiques of cross-cultural research methods focus on the pitfalls of utilizing assessment instruments with culturally-different groups that have been developed and normed in Western cultural settings. This section will present several of the key challenges raised in the cross-cultural research literature that can compromise measurement validity or equivalence of such complex constructs as "depression." These include content equivalence, semantic equivalence, and technical equivalence (Flaherty, Gaviria, Pathak, Mitchell, Wintrob, Richman, & Birz, 1988).

Content equivalence. One dimension of cross-cultural equivalence that must be considered when measuring depression is the extent to which the content of each item of an instrument is relevant to the phenomenon under investigation in the cultural context of those being studied. This often involves item-by-item scrutiny by a team of multicultural social scientists and indigenous cultural experts (Flaherty et al., 1988). For example, scale items that may be culture-bound to mainstream American society, such as questions pertaining to antisocial behavior or suicidal ideation (Flaherty et al., 1988), or to such psychological terms as guilt or remorse (Jenkins, Kleinman, & Good, 1991), may not be recognized as meaningful or relevant by members of the particular cultural group being studied. In such cases, cross-cultural researchers recommend eliminating or replacing items of questionable content equivalence. However, if a number of key questionnaire items are deleted or modified, the internal consistency of the measure can be so compromised as to require the search for or development of a new instrument (Flaherty et al., 1988; Munet-Vilaró, & Egan, 1990).

Semantic equivalence. Another form of equivalence important to cross-cultural measurement validity is the meaning of each item after translation into the language or vernacular of the respondents. Back-translation is often the strategy of choice when preparing an instrument developed in English to be administered to respondents who speak another language (Flaherty et al., 1988). This is a time-consuming process whereby panels of bilingual experts (1) translate the instrument from language A to language B, (2) translate it back from language B to language A, (3) examine each item on both versions for meaning uniformity, and (4) reword or eliminate items viewed as having different meanings (Brislin, 1970). While simply rewording an item may be sufficient to achieve meaning congruence in some cases, often the vernacular of North American assessment instruments is difficult to translate into other languages (Kleinman, 1987). This is especially true of such terms or idioms as *feeling blue, downhearted,* or *downtrodden,* that are often included in standard measures of depression. Thus, even when cultural idioms of distress are correctly back-translated, they may be mismatched in terms of metaphorical meaning. For example, a study of the mental health status of Laotian Hmong adolescent refugees in the U.S. reported considerable difficulties in matching figurative expressions for psychological attitudes and affective states between English and Hmong lexicon (Dunnigan, McNall, & Mortimer, 1993). These researchers found that the Hmong youth also employed metaphor when communicating emotions, but, in contrast to youth in the general population, the Hmong analogies referred to various states of "difficult liver" brought on by specific precipitating events. For instance, to have a "lonely liver" is to feel separated from loved ones or abandoned; and a "destroyed liver" means that one is feeling completely discouraged.

Even well-assimilated Americans who represent culturally-diverse backgrounds can be muddled or put-off by English-language phrases or idioms that do not reflect how they typically view the world or express themselves. Thus, problems of semantic nonequivalence in standardized measures can also occur among respondents who speak English, but for whom certain "common" or "standard" figures of speech or "tropes" do not convey the meaning intended by those who developed the instrument. For instance, cultural consultants in a study of social support characteristics among African-American and Filipino-American parents, suggested changing some words and phrases in several standardized measures to enhance reliable and valid responding (Richey, Hodges, Agbayani-Siewert, & Petitt, in press). These included changing "I feel like a wallflower when I go out" to "I feel like people don't notice me when I go out" on the Index of Self-Esteem, and "My family gets on my nerves" to "My family upsets me" on the Index of Family Relations (Hudson, 1982). Minor changes were also made in several items on the Perceived Social Support scale (Procidano & Heller, 1983). For instance, the item, "My family gives me the moral support I need" was altered to "My family helps me to feel hopeful."

Another subtle, but perhaps important, semantic consideration that can influence measurement validity, is the choice of verbs used with certain psychological or emotional states. For example, respondents may react differentially to questions cast in affective terms ("how do you feel about . . . ") versus questions phrased in cognitive terms ("what do you think about . . . ") (Ponterotto & Casas, 1991). This possibility raises some interesting questions about a number of measures frequently utilized in clinical studies of depression that often include items that reflect a mixture of cognitive appraisal and affect. For instance, while some items suggest a cognitive state–I think I am as good as other people, I believe I look ugly, I have lost interest in others, I am critical of myself–other items appear to convey an emotional state–I feel like I am as good as other people, I feel unattractive, I feel appreciated by others, I feel others disapprove of me. The extent to which these subtle linguistic features in standard instruments might compromise validity among culturally diverse respondents, who also differ by gender, is unknown.

Technical equivalence. Another challenge to measurement validity in cross-cultural research is the method of data collection, including how data are obtained (self-report questionnaire or interview), and the format and scaling of instruments. A number of cross-cultural researchers believe that paper-and-pencil instruments routinely introduce bias into data collected in non-Western cultures, where individuals may be unfamiliar with or suspicious of written-response questionnaires, have minimal literacy levels, or be irritated or offended by repetitious, probing, or negatively-worded questions (e.g., Flaherty et al., 1988; Kinzie & Manson, 1987). In some societies, indigenous research methods implicitly censor more formal interview formats, including questionnaires. For example, in the Philippines, *pagtatanong-tanong* or "asking questions" is the recommended research method for gathering information (Pe-Pua, 1989). *Pagtatanong-tanong* emphasizes a relaxed and friendly interaction or dialogue between status equals that is characterized by mutual exploration and discussion. Clearly, this format is very different from the usual researcher-subject interview protocol of one-way information exchange.

Many of the criticisms and cautions raised by cross-cultural researchers can be levied against self-report data formats when used to collect information from relatively assimilated Americans who represent diverse racial/ethnic backgrounds. For instance, items on paper-and-pencil instruments may be read to respondents because literacy levels are perceived or assessed as minimal, or because English is a second or third language. While this is often an acceptable substitute for self-administration, the effects of reading self-report instruments to clients or subjects remain relatively unstudied (Kinzie & Manson, 1987). Given that some segments of the population (e.g., women and Hispanics) may be more likely to respond in ways that elicit social approval (Vernon, Roberts, & Lee, 1982), the reliability and validity of results from questionnaires administered orally or interactively might be further compromised among these populations when compared with data collected "privately" through self-administration.

Assessing technical equivalence also involves considering different response tendencies among cultural groups and the impact of common strategies in many standardized measures to counter these (Flaherty et al., 1988). For instance, in addition to observations that some cultural groups tend to respond with "yes" to survey questions (Roberts & Vernon, 1984), other researchers acknowledge problems with extreme response sets (Jenkins, Kleinman, & Good, 1991; Marin & Marin, 1991; Uehara et al., 1996), and trait desirability (Dunnigan et al., 1993). This latter tendency, trait desirability, influences responses to questions that represent highly desirable or undesirable characteristics in a particular culture. For example, cultural norms prohibit Hmong adults from endorsing statements that might portray them as self-important and arrogant, or conversely, as weak and vulnerable, especially as these admissions might reflect on and bring shame to the extended family (Dunnigan et al., 1993).

To counter these response tendencies, standardized instruments often incorporate questions or scaling formats that identify or adjust for acquiescence, extreme answers, or trait desirability. Unfortunately, these corrective strategies, such as providing more response gradations (e.g., replacing nominal or "true-false" response options with multiple-point Likert scales), repeating questions, and mixing positive and negative items, can introduce additional challenges to technical equivalence with culturally diverse groups. For instance, Vietnamese mental health workers recommended a 3-point response scale over a 5-point scale in a depression measure because they believed. respondents were less aware than Caucasian middle-class Americans of internal affective nuances (Kinzie & Manson, 1987). Similarly, the common practice of rewording or repeating the same questions in an instrument may be perceived as coercive, cumbersome, and rude by respondents whose culture values reticence and courteousness (Flaherty et al., 1988). Finally, although mixing positive and negative items in a questionnaire can deter response set, negatively worded items can present significant translation and interpretation problems that can result in data of questionable accuracy (e.g., Munet-Vilaró & Egan, 1990).

RECOMMENDATIONS

As the foregoing discussion suggests, the lack of agreement about and specification of the expression of depressive symptoms across different ethnic minority women require social work researchers to cautiously assess the utility of strategies, including the use of standardized instruments, to measure this complex and elusive construct. As noted, there is considerable variability among American ethnic minorities, especially among women of color, in the factor structures of depression measures normed on mainstream Caucasian populations. Current critics attribute many of these differences to language and instrument biases, which are influenced by difficulties encountered in the translation process (e.g., Callahan & Wolinsky, 1994; Marin & Marin, 1993). As noted, measures may be semantically or linguistically equivalent, but still fail to capture the construct of interest as this is uniquely expressed in a particular cultural group.

We agree with Kleinman (1987, p. 453) who encourages researchers to exercise "humility in the face of alternative cultural formulations of human problems" and to feel "uncomfortable with our taken-for-granted professional categories . . . " To this we would add the importance of constant introspection or self-reflection by researchers about how discrepancies in power, status and influence between themselves and "the researched" can promote distorted communication and false conclusions (Uehara et al., 1996). Along with these general admonitions to applied social scientists, we offer several recommendations that could promote more culturally-sensitive and culturally-valid methods in social work research with women of color who experience "depression" in multiple ways. Specifically, we offer suggestions for promoting methodological diversity, enhancing the cross-cultural equivalence of self-report measures, expanding assessment to consider environmental risk and resiliency factors, attending to the interpersonal processes of data collection, and engaging in researcher self-assessment.

Methodological diversity. One overarching recommendation offered by cross-cultural researchers is methodological diversity–the utilization of multiple research methodologies simultaneously or in coordinated seque-

lae that subsequently link and integrate qualitative and quantitative procedures (Ponterotto & Casas, 1991). Various methodologic combinations
can be achieved by incorporating different sources of and procedures for
collecting data, in multiple contexts (Jenkins, Kleinman, & Good, 1991).
Multiple methods and multisource strategies allow researchers to critically
assess for triangulation or congruency in meaning among various sources
of information. When information from different venues appears congru-
ent, confidence in the validity of study findings is enhanced.

Social work researchers can achieve multimethod and multisource measures in studies with culturally-diverse groups by: (1) sampling various
response modes, including indicators of somatic, interpersonal-familial,
and psycho-emotional-spiritual distress; (2) employing a mix of standardized instruments, client- or population-specific questions or scales with
options for open-ended answers, self-monitoring or diary formats, individual and group interviews, and field or in-vivo observations; (3) representing the viewpoints of respondents themselves in addition to those of relevant figures or key informants in the respondent's family or community;
and (4) gathering information from different contexts or situations in
which respondents typically function.

Cross-cultural equivalency. When selecting or developing measures for
research with people who represent ethnic/cultural minority groups, social
work scholars would likely benefit from reviewing relevant cross-cultural
literature in other disciplines, and from ongoing consultation with bilingual and bicultural experts in the communities of interest. For example,
much has been written by cross-cultural scholars about procedures for
examining an existing instrument for conceptual and linguistic equivalency, adapting or translating a measure for use with specific populations, and
creating and validating new scales (e.g., Dunningan, McNall, & Mortimer,
1993; Flaherty et al., 1988; Kinzie & Manson, 1987; Munet-Vilaró &
Egan, 1990; Ponterotto & Casas, 1991). Some of these suggestions include: (1) detailed steps for translating an inventory from the original
language to the language of the target population; (2) useful examples of
culture-specific idioms that were identified through ethnographic methods, which subsequently replaced more ethnocentric tropes on standardized forms; and (3) guidelines for pilot testing tailored measures on a small
subset (e.g., 5%) of the eventual sample, including asking respondents for
feedback on measurement content, format, and process.

An additional consideration in assuring measurement equivalence is
assessing the extent to which individuals from differing racial, ethnic,
cultural, and socioeconomic backgrounds actually differ from the major-
ity-group in views and values. While errors are often made by overlooking

these important differences, presuming that such differences exist simply because an individual presents or appears as a person from a racial/ethnic minority background could be equally problematic. Thus, before altering standardized instruments to be more culture-specific, it is important to assess such factors as worldview, levels of acculturation into American society, and racial-ethnic identity (Sabnani & Ponterotto, 1992). For example, language usage is but one of several dimensions of acculturation. Other dimensions can include language familiarity, ethnic pride and identity, level of co-ethnic interaction, and proximity to kin. One available instrument developed to assess acculturation levels is the Acculturation Rating Scale for Mexican Americans (ARSMA) (Cuellar, Harris, & Jasso, 1980). In their critical review of 8 racial/ethnic minority-specific instruments, Sabnani and Ponterotto (1992) report that the ARSMA is fairly well-established and has adequate evidence of reliability and validity.

In addition to these valuable recommendations by cross-cultural researchers, we would suggest greater attention to more creative forms of scaling in measures bound for multicultural use. For instance, visual analogue scales (VAS) and other forms of symbolic measurement, may be useful in addressing format anxiety that can compromise reliability of numbered scales (e.g., Flaherty et al., 1988). Unlike a numbered scale, a VAS presents a 10-centimeter, unnumbered line anchored by terms that reflect the variable of interest, for example, "extremely depressed" and "not at all depressed" (Aitken, 1969). This scale format allows persons to mark on the line their current states. A "score" is determined by measuring the number of centimeters between one anchor and the respondent's mark. In addition to evidence that the VAS has psychometric reliability and validity as a measure of depression (Aitken, 1969; Teasdale & Fennell, 1982), these scales have also been successfully utilized with diverse clients and research participants for whom linguistic, educational, attentional, and perceptual factors can compromise data collection using more conventional numerical scaling formats (e.g., Richey et al., in press; Richey, Lovell, & Reid, 1991; Richey, Kopp, Tolson, & Ishisaka, 1987).

Although untested, these scales could also be anchored by visual depictions or symbols of positive-negative affective states that are culturally and/or individually specific, thus eliminating the need for written words altogether. Such scales could also be anchored by culturally-specific metaphors or figurative language that reflect deeply-imbedded cultural beliefs. For example, the use of *dichos* or Latino figurative language has been suggested as a therapeutic method for enhancing rapport, altering perceptions of problems and solutions, and addressing culturally-based resistance (Zuñiga, 1992). Conceivably, some abbreviated forms of *dichos* could be used as VAS anchors in measures of depression with Latinas.

Risk and resiliency factors. Current assessment and measurement protocols give relatively little attention to environmental–risk or resiliency–factors as they may relate to depression. This oversight is understandable to some extent, given that current American psychiatric conceptualizations and diagnoses of depression tend to focus on psychobiological responses or symptoms, and do not adequately take into account overall life stress nor level of coping or adaptation achieved by people given their environmental realities.

Omitting consideration of environmental factors in assessment and measurement activities is especially problematic for women of color since there appear to be significant socio-environmental correlates or stressors that relate to the presence or severity of depression. For example, research suggests that single-parenthood, lack of social support, low socioeconomic status, unemployment, and living in unsafe environments are factors associated with higher risk for depression among women of color (e.g., Barbee, 1992; Brown, 1990; Jambunathan, 1992; Kizilay, 1992; Tabora & Falskerud, 1994; Warren, 1994). By including systematic consideration of contextual factors that are known to be correlated with depression, researchers may be more regularly cued to assess for the presence and severity of dysphoria, demoralization, and hopelessness among women of color, thus decreasing the likelihood of false negative results.

One possible remedy to current symptom-only measurement approaches is adapting the Person-In-Environment (PIE) classification system to social work research activities. The PIE was developed for use in social work practice settings and differs from traditional psychiatric diagnosis of mental disease by focusing attention on social role functioning, environmental barriers and supports, and client coping skills (Karls & Wandrei, 1992). For example, the recently-published PIE Manual includes consideration of a large number of environmental factors that are potentially relevant in assessing depression among women of color, e.g., health and safety factors such as living and working in unsafe or violent conditions; discrimination in employment, education, housing, health and social services; and availability of affectional support systems (Karls & Wandrei, 1994a, 1994b). Although the PIE system is relatively new and untested, especially as it may relate to measurement activities in practice and research domains, it nonetheless holds promise for expanding attention to variables of interest beyond those that are largely psychological, and hence, more prone to ethnocentric bias.

Process and context of data collection. In addition to attending to the content and equivalence of measurement tools, and expanding assessment to include consideration of environmental variables associated with depression, it is also important to think about how information will be collected. Cross-cultural researchers often point out that the sequence, pace, and social etiquette of the assessment process is as critical to the quality and completeness of the data collected as are decisions about instrumentation (e.g., Flaherty et al., 1988; Pe-Pua, 1989). Several data collection processes and procedures should be considered. First, how will researchers negotiate entry into the study community and establish rapport and trust with participants (Milburn, Gary, Booth, & Brown, 1991)? Some have suggested the utility of consulting or collaborating with individuals indigenous to the community of interest who can assist with entry as well as with data collection and interpretation (Pe-Pua, 1989; Tapp, Kelman, Triandis, Wrightsman, & Coelho, 1974, as reprinted in Ponterotto, Casas, Suzuki, & Alexander, 1995).

Second, where and how will information be collected? Will data be gathered through individual, in-home interviews with women and their families, or with groups of women in community or neighborhood settings? For example, a study of social support characteristics among African-American and Filipino-American parents collected data during home-based interviews to accommodate respondents' work and family schedules, child-care responsibilities, and to promote a more informal and friendly atmosphere, which often included small talk, opportunities for dialogue and mutual disclosure, and the serving of food to interviewers (Richey et al., 1996). Decisions about where and how data will be collected also need to consider how interviewer and respondent gender may influence cross-gender interactions within particular cultural contexts. For example, cross-cultural researchers caution female interviewers about the consequences of conducting informal, one-to-one interviews with male informants, because the informant may feel uncomfortable and become the target of community suspicion, and the community's regard for the researcher will be compromised (Pe-Pua, 1989). In developing countries, male researchers are often discouraged from conducting private interviews of women (Flaherty et al., 1988).

Third, what will be the order, combination, and pace of assessment activities? To enhance reliability and validity of information, cross-cultural experts stress the importance of including a "warm up" period in data collection procedures that may be accomplished by a free response format for gathering initial demographic information (Flaherty et al., 1988). Others recommend continued flexibility throughout the process to allow for researcher self-disclosure and respondent elaboration or "talk story" (Pe-Pua, 1989). Initial selection of topics that focus on less sensitive issues as well as on individual, family, or cultural strengths may also facilitate and accelerate respondent comfort and motivation to participate. Respondent openness and involvement may be further facilitated by introducing activities or topics initially that are more interactive or activity-based, such as mapping out or drawing one's family tree or social network on large sheets of paper, storytelling, or creating personalized cards for a card sort activity. Assessment and measurement activities that encourage active participant involvement and dissuade passivity and compliance may be especially important in research with depressed women of color. In this way, data collection procedures can also serve as an empowerment tool, in addition to providing potentially useful information (Kopp, 1989).

Researcher self-assessment. Finally, we believe it is important for social work researchers to assess their own levels of cultural competence as they embark on and sustain research activity with individuals and communities of color. We support the position that "good" multicultural social work research is a reflective and collaborative process, the ultimate goal of which is social transformation (Uehara et al., in press). With this definition in mind, successful cross-cultural research requires a plethora of competencies, including skills in introspection, cultural analysis, critical and historical reflection, cross-cultural communication, and democratic or egalitarian decision-making (Uehara et al., in press). Admittedly, these competencies may be relatively new to social work *research* endeavors, but they are not new to social work *practice.* Although more attention has been focused on articulating multicultural competencies, guidelines, and standards for service providers or practitioners, many of these principles and self-assessment tools appear very relevant to social work researchers (e.g., Ponterotto, Casas, Suzuki, & Alexander, 1995; Sabnani & Ponterotto, 1992). For example, cross-cultural counselor characteristics include: (1) self-awareness of one's own assumptions, values, and biases; (2) understanding of the worldviews of culturally different clients; (3) developing and practicing appropriate interventions for culturally-different clients (Sue, Arredondo, & McDavis, 1992, as reprinted in Ponterotto et al., 1995). For each of these three general counselor characteristics, Sue and associates further articulate three dimensions: attitudes and beliefs, knowledge, and skills. With these added dimensions, a nine-cell matrix of cross-cultural skills can be organized. Such a matrix could potentially be adapted for use by cross-cultural researchers who could employ it as a checklist of sorts for purposes of ongoing self-monitoring. Since most cross-cultural experts stress that becoming culturally competent is an active, ongoing process that never ends (Sue & Sue, 1990), it is important that social work researchers develop or select self-assessment strategies that promote regular and sustained self-observation and self-correction. For instance, Green (1995) offers a number of practical strategies and exercises to help social workers expand their cross-cultural capabilities. One of these, self-observation through diaries or checklists (e.g., Kopp, 1989), is suggested as a useful tool to advance self-awareness of one's emotional, behavioral, and attitudinal responses in cross-cultural situations.

Just as the profession encourages social work practitioners to assess their competencies and effectiveness, so, too, must social work researchers critically evaluate their competencies–their attitudes, knowledge, and skills–and their effectiveness in contributing to "good" multicultural research processes and outcomes. This mandate for researcher self-assessment and self-correction is especially important in areas of cross-cultural inquiry where the waters are relatively uncharted and murky, and the charts that do exist have been penned by navigators in other disciplines who have done most of their exploring in international waters.

CONCLUSION

While the literature on cross-cultural research methodology has largely come from disciplines other than social work, we believe social work researchers can contribute much to understanding the causes, correlates, and "cures" of depression among culturally-diverse individuals, especially women of color. The growing emphasis on and interest in culturally-competent and gender-relevant practice, along with our professional values of social justice, equality, and empowerment, support the foundation for our optimism. This article has pinpointed and exemplified some of the challenges that await multicultural researchers, and has offered a number of possible remedies for addressing and minimizing these. We hope the discussion generates further examination of these challenges and remedies, as well as yet unarticulated caveats and creative solutions.

REFERENCES

Aitken, R.C.B. (1969). Measurement of feelings using visual analogue scales. *Proceedings of the Royal Society of Medicine, 62*, 989-993.
Barbee, E.L. (1992). African American women and depression: A review and critique of the literature. *Archives of Psychiatric Nursing, 6*, 257-265.
Barbee, E.L. (1994). Healing time: The blues and African-American women. *Health Care for Women International, 15*, 53-60.
Beiser, M. (1985). A study of depression among traditional Africans, urban North Americans, and southeast Asian refugees. In A. Kleinman & B. Good (Eds.),

Culture and depression (pp. 272-293). Berkeley: University of California Press, Ltd.

Breslau, N. (1985). Depressive symptoms, major depression, and generalized anxiety: A comparison of self-reports on CES-D and results from diagnostic interviews. *Psychiatry Research, 15*, 219-229.

Brislin, R.W. (1970). Back-translation for cross-cultural research. *Journal of Cross-Cultural Psychology, 1*, 185-216.

Brown, D.R. (1990). Depression among Blacks: An epidemiologic perspective. In D. S. Ruiz (Ed.), *Handbook of mental health and mental disorder among Black Americans*. Westport: Greenwood Press.

Callahan, C.M., & Wolinsky, F.D. (1994). The effect of gender and race on measurement properties of the CES-D in older adults. *Medical Care, 32*, 341-356.

Canino, G.J., Rubio-Stipec, M., Shrout, P.E., Milagros, B., Stolberg, R., & Bird, H.R. (1987). Sex differences and depression in Puerto Rico. *Psychology of Women Quarterly, 11*, 443-459.

Chang, W.C. (1985). A cross-cultural study of depressive symptomology. *Culture, Medicine & Psychiatry, 9*, 295-317.

Cuellar, I., Harris, L.C., & Jasso, R. (1980). An acculturation scale for Mexican-American normal and clinical populations. *Hispanic Journal of Behavioral Sciences, 2*, 199-217.

Dunnigan, T., McNall, M., & Mortimer, J.T. (1993). The problem of metaphorical nonequivalence in cross-cultural survey research: Comparing the mental health statuses of Hmong refugee and general population adolescents. *Journal of Cross-Cultural Psychology, 24*, 344-365.

Escobar, J.I., Gomes, J., & Tuason, V.B. (1983). Depressive phenomenology in North and South American patients. *American Journal of Psychiatry, 140*, 47-51.

Flaherty, J.A., Gaviria, F.M., Pathak, D., Mitchell, T., Wintrob, R., Richman, J.A., & Birz, S. (1988). Developing instruments for cross-cultural psychiatric research. *The Journal of Nervous and Mental Disease, 176*, 257-263.

Franks, F., & Faux, S.A. (1990). Depression, stress, mastery, and social resources in four ethnocultural women's groups. *Research in Nursing & Health, 13*, 282-292.

Goleman, D. (1992, December 8, 1992). A rising cost of modernity: Depression. *The New York Times*, pp. C1.

Green, J.W. (1995). *Cultural awareness in the human services: A multi-ethnic approach* (Second Edition). Boston: Allyn and Bacon.

Guarnaccia, P.J., Angel, R., & Worobey, J.L. (1989). The factor structure of the CES-D in the Hispanic Health and Nutrition Examination Survey: The influences of ethnicity, gender, and language. *Social Science and Medicine, 29*, 85-94.

Hudson, W.W. (1982). *The clinical measurement package: A field manual*. Homewood, IL: The Dorsey Press.

Jambunathan, J. (1992). Sociocultural factors in depression in Asian Indian women. *Health Care for Women International, 13*, 261-270.

Jenkins, J.H., Kleinman, A., & Good, B.J. (1991). Cross-cultural studies in depression. In J. Becker & A. Kleinman (Eds.), *Psychosocial aspects of depression* (pp. 67-99). Hillsdale, NJ: L. Erlbaum Associates.

Karls, J.M., & Wandrei, K.E. (1992). PIE: A new language for social work. *Social Work, 37,* 80-85.

Karls, J.M., & Wandrei, K.E. (Eds.) (1994a). *Person-In-Environment system: The PIE classification system for social functioning problems.* Washington, DC: NASW Press.

Karls, J.M., & Wandrei, K.E. (1994b). *PIE manual: Person-In-Environment system.* Washington, DC: NASW Press.

Kinzie, J.D., & Manson, S.M. (1987). The use of self-rating scales in cross-cultural psychiatry. *Hospital and Community Psychiatry, 38,* 190-196.

Kizilay, P.E. (1992). Predictors of depression in women. *Nursing Clinics of North America, 27,* 983-993.

Kleinman, A. (1987). Anthropology and psychiatry: The role of culture in cross-cultural research on illness. *British Journal of Psychiatry, 151,* 447-454.

Kleinman, A., & Good, B. (Eds.). (1985a). *Culture and depression.* Berkeley: University of California Press.

Kleinman, A., & Good, B. (1985b). Introduction: Culture and depression. In A. Kleinman & B. Good (Eds.), *Culture and depression* (pp. 1-33). Berkeley: University of California Press, Ltd.

Kleinman, A., & Kleinman, J. (1985). Somatization: The interconnections in Chinese society among culture, depressive experiences, and the meanings of pain. In A. Kleinman & B. Good (Eds.), *Culture and depression* (pp. 429-490). Berkeley: University of California Press, Ltd.

Kopp, J. (1989). Self-observation: An empowerment strategy in assessment. *Social Casework, 70,* 276-284.

Landrum-Brown, J. (1990). Black mental health and racial oppression. In D.S. Ruiz (Ed.), *Handbook of mental health and mental disorder among Black Americans.* Westport: Greenwood Press.

Lin, N., & Dean, A. (1984). Social support and depression. *Social Psychiatry, 1984,* 83-91.

Marin, G., & Marin, B.V. (1991). *Research with Hispanic populations* (Vol. 23). Newbury Park: Sage Publications.

Markides, K.S., & Farrell, J. (1985). Marital status and depression among Mexican Americans. *Social Psychiatry, 20,* 86-91.

Munet-Vilaró, F., & Egan, M. (1990). Reliability issues of the Family Environment Scale for cross-cultural research. *Nursing Research, 39,* 244-247.

Napholz, L. (1994). Dysphoria among Hispanic working women: A research note. *Hispanic Journal of Behavioral Sciences, 16,* 500-509.

Pe-Pua, R. (1989). Pagtatanong-Tanong: A cross-cultural research method. *International Journal of Intercultural Relations, 13,* 147-163.

Ponterotto, J.G. & Casas, J.M. (1991). *Handbook of racial/ethnic minority counseling research.* Springfield, IL.: Charles C Thomas.

Ponterotto, J.G., Casas, J.M., Suzuki, L.A., & Alexander, C.M. (Eds.) (1995). *Handbook of multicultural counseling.* Thousand Oaks, CA: Sage.

Procidano, M.E., & Heller, K. (1983). Measures of perceived social support from friends and family: Three validation studies. *American Journal of Community Psychology, 11,* 1 -24.

Radloff, L.S. (1977). The CES-D Scale: A self-report depression scale for research in the general population. *Applied Psychological Measurement, 1,* 385-401.

Richey, C.A., Hodges, V.G., Agbayani-Siewert, P., & Petitt, K. (1996). Social support characteristics among nonclinical African-American and Filipino-American parents with school-age children. *Children and Youth Services Review, 18,* 659-692.

Richey, C.A., Kopp, J., Tolson, E.R., & Ishisaka, H.A. (1987). Practice evaluation in diverse settings. In N. Gottlieb, H.A. Ishisaka, J. Kopp, C.A. Richey, & E.R. Tolson (Eds.), *Perspectives on direct practice evaluation* (pp. 153-170). Seattle: Center for Social Welfare Research.

Richey, C.A., Lovell, M.L., & Reid, K. (1991). Interpersonal skill training to enhance social support among women at risk for child maltreatment. *Children and Youth Services Review, 13,* 41-59.

Roberts, R.E. (1987). Epidemiological issues in measuring preventive effects. In R.F. Muñoz (Ed.), *Depression prevention research directions* (pp. 45-68). New York: Hemisphere Publishing Corporation.

Roberts, R.E., Rhoades, H.M., & Vernon, S.W. (1990). Using the CES-D scale to screen for depression and anxiety: Effects of language and ethnic status. *Psychiatric Research, 31,* 69-83.

Roberts, R.E., & Vernon, S.W. (1983). The Center for Epidemiologic studies Depression Scale: Its use in a community sample. *American Journal of Psychiatry, 140,* 41-45.

Roberts, R.E., Vernon, S.W., & Rhoades, H.M. (1989). Effects of language and ethnic status on reliability and validity of the Center for Epidemiologic Studies-Depression Scale with psychiatric patients. *Nervous and Mental Disease, 177,* 581-592.

Rodrigues-Gomez, J.R. (1993). *Family structure and depression: A study of Puerto Rican women in New York.* New York: Fordham University.

Runck, B. (1986). NIMH to launch major campaign on recognition and treatment of depression. *Hospital and Community Psychiatry, 37,* 779-788.

Sabnani, H.H., & Ponterotto, J.G. (1992). Racial/ethnic minority-specific instrumentation in counseling research: A review, critique, and recommendations. *Measurement and Evaluation in Counseling and Development, 24,* 161-187.

Sartorius, N., Jablensky, W., Gulbinat, W., & Ernberg, G. (1980). WHO collaborative study: Assessment of depressive disorders. *Psychological Medicine, 10,* 743-749.

Schwartz, A., & Schwartz, R.M. (1993). *Depression: Theories and treatments: Psychological, biological, and social perspectives.* New York: Columbia University Press.

Sheppard, M. (1994). Maternal depression, child care and the social work role. *British Journal of Social Work, 24,* 33-51.

Shin, K.R. (1994). Psychosocial predictors of depressive symptoms in Korean-American women in New York City. *Women & Health, 21,* 73-82.

Song, Y.I. (1991). Single Asian American women as a result of divorce: Depressive affect and changes in social support. *Journal of Divorce & Remarriage, 14,* 219-230.

Stroup-Benham, C.A., Lawrence, R.H., & Trevino, F.M. (1989). CES-D factor structure among Mexican American and Puerto Rican women from single- and couple-headed households. *Hispanic Journal of Behavioral Sciences, 14,* 310-326.

Sue, D.W., Arredondo, P., & McDavis, R. (1992). Multicultural counseling competencies and standards: A call to the profession. *Journal of Counseling and Development, 70,* 477-486.

Sue, D.W., & Sue, D. (1990). *Counseling the culturally different: Theory and practice.* New York: Wiley.

Tabora, B., & Flaskerud, J.H. (1994). Depression among Chinese Americans: Review of the literature. *Issues in Mental Health Nursing, 15,* 569-584.

Tapp, J.L., Kelman, H., Triandis, H., Wrightsman, L., & Coelho, G. (1974). Advisory principals for ethical consideration in the conduct of cross-cultural research: Fall 1973 revision. *International Journal of Psychology, 9,* 240-249.

Teasdale, J.D., & Fennel, J.B. (1982). Immediate effects on depression of cognitive interventions. *Cognitive Therapy and Research, 6,* 343-351.

Thornicroft, G., & Sartorius, N. (1993). The course and outcome of depression in different cultures: 10-year follow-up of the WHO collaborative study on the assessment of depressive disorders. *Psychological Medicine, 23,* 1023-1032.

Uehara, E., Sohng, S.S.L., Bending, R.L., Seyfried, S., Richey, C.A., Spencer, M., Morelli, P., Ortega, D.M., Keenan, L.D., & Kanuha, V. (1996). Towards a values-based approach to multicultural social work research. *Social Work, 41,* 613-621.

Vega, W.A., Kolody, B., & Valle, J.R. (1986). The relationship of marital status, confidant support and depression among Mexican immigrant women. *Journal of Marriage and Family, 48,* 597-605.

Vernon, S.W., Roberts, R.E., & Lee, E.S. (1982). Response tendencies, ethnicity, and depression scores. *American Journal of Epidemiology, 116,* 482-495.

Warren, B.J. (1994). Depression in African-American women. *Journal of Psychosocial Nursing, 32,* 29-33.

Wetzel, J.W. (1978). Depression and dependence upon unsustaining environments. *Clinical Social Work Journal, 6,* 75-87.

Wetzel, J. W. (1984). *Clinical handbook of depression.* New York: Gardner Press.

Wetzel, J. W. (1994). Depression: Women-at-risk. *Social Work in Health Care, 19,* 85-108.

Wortman, R.A. (1981). Depression, danger, dependency, denial: Work with poor, black, single parents. *American Journal of Orthopsychiatry, 51,* 662-671.

Zuñiga, M.E. (1992). Using metaphors in therapy: *Dichos* and Latino clients. *Social Work, 37,* 55-60.

Conceptual and Methodological Considerations in Research with Non-White Ethnic Elders

Denise Burnette

EDITORS' NOTE. This comprehensive presentation of issues arising in research with ethnic minority elders yields the following generalizable research principles and suggestions for future research: (1) The political factors that have influenced existing nomenclatures and taxonomies, such as ethnic classifications, need to be identified by the researcher, as they will influence subsequent problem definitions and methodological choices. (2) Measurement equivalence needs to be established at several levels–conceptual, metric, and structural. As noted by the author, this requires the application of particular methodological and statistical strategies such as multitrait-multimethod analyses, triangulation, and structural equation modeling. Although these are well-established techniques, they have infrequently been applied to cross-cultural measurement problems. (3) Researchers should be wary of making cross-cultural comparisons based on participant self-ratings, as such ratings are made in relation to the participants' reference groups, which will differ across cultures. In other words, so-called etic interpretations cannot be ascribed to fundamentally emic phenomena. (4) As noted in this article and elsewhere in this volume, quantitative and qualitative methods should both be employed to provide complementary and comprehensive data. (5) In order to minimize sampling bias and ensure adequate

Denise Burnette is affiliated with the Columbia University School of Social Work, 622 West 113th Street, New York, NY 10025.

[Haworth co-indexing entry note]: "Conceptual and Methodological Considerations in Research with Non-White Ethnic Elders." Burnette, Denise. Co-published simultaneously in *Journal of Social Service Research* (The Haworth Press, Inc.) Vol. 23, No. 3/4, 1998, pp. 71-91; and: *Social Work Research with Minority and Oppressed Populations: Methodological Issues and Innovations* (ed: Miriam Potocky and Antoinette Y. Rodgers-Farmer) The Haworth Press, Inc., 1998, pp. 71-91. Single or multiple copies of this article are available for a fee from The Haworth Document Delivery Service [1-800-342-9678, 9:00 a.m. - 5:00 p.m. (EST). E-mail address: getinfo@haworth.com].

representation of minority groups, specialized sampling strategies are required. Disproportionate stratified random sampling is the best method in this regard. Since stratification must be applied to several variables simultaneously (for example, ethnicity, age, socioeconomic status), this will require access to large populations. Because such access is beyond the resources of most individual researchers, investigators need to advocate for more specialized sampling (as well as expanded data collection) in the various national surveys conducted by the federal government. (6) The "life review," a therapeutic method that is widely used with elders, needs to be further investigated in regard to its utility and validity as a research tool. (7) Finally, the life course perspective discussed by the author provides another example of an expanded conceptual framework that would be expected to yield a more comprehensive and insightful understanding of participants' experiences.

SUMMARY. Due to greater longevity and recent waves of immigration, growth rates for ethnic minority elders are expected to far exceed those of same-aged whites in the next half century. Yet, research in social gerontology has focused almost exclusively on older whites. This paper addresses conceptual and methodological issues relevant to research on nonwhite ethnic elders. The rationale for clear, consistent terminology to define and target study populations is presented first, followed by theoretical and conceptual issues, particularly as they relate to measurement for and across different racial, ethnic, and cultural groups. Finally, issues related to quantitative and qualitative design, data collection, and analysis are discussed. *[Article copies available for a fee from The Haworth Document Delivery Service: 1-800-342-9678. E-mail address: getinfo@haworth.com]*

BACKGROUND: DIVERSITY OF AGING POPULATION

Since 1900, the percentage of Americans age 65 and over has more than tripled (4.1% in 1900 to 12.7% in 1994), and their numbers have increased nearly eleven times (from 3.1 million to 33.2 million). This growth is expected to continue, then accelerate between 2010, when the "baby boom" generation begins to reach late life, and 2030, when one in five Americans will be age 65 or over. As a result of greater longevity and recent waves of immigration, growth rates for ethnic minority elders are expected to far exceed those of same-aged whites. Between 1990 and

2030, the white non-Hispanic aged population is projected to increase by 93%, compared to 328% for older ethnic minorities, including Hispanics (555%), non-Hispanic blacks (160%), American Indians, Eskimos, and Aleuts (231%), and Asians and Pacific Islanders (693%) (American Association of Retired Persons, 1995).

Research in social gerontology has focused almost exclusively on older whites, who in 1990 represented nearly 90% of persons aged 65 and over. As a result, theory development and the application of sophisticated research methods to the study of aging among ethnic and minority populations have lagged (Markides, Liang, & Jackson, 1990). Moreover, much of the research on these populations has involved retrofitting methods of inquiry to already established dominant patterns of aging (Bastida, 1987) and emphasizing minority status and its attendant disadvantages at the expense of understanding the broader concepts of race, ethnicity, and culture in the aging process (American Psychiatric Association, 1994; Markides, Liang, & Jackson, 1990).

Ethnogerontology, an evolving field of aging research, aims to address such conceptual and methodological shortcomings by examining the aging process in the context of the lived experiences of racial and ethnic subgroups of older adults (Jackson & Ensley, 1990-91; Usui, 1989). Comparative studies show substantial variation within and among these groups on crucial indicators of well-being, including economic security, health status and health care, mental health, family life, and social supports (Levine, 1982; Padgett, 1995; Taueber, 1990). Additional research is needed to specify the influence of factors such as language; cultural beliefs, norms, and values; minority, socioeconomic, and immigration statuses; and geographic locale on differential well-being among older ethnic groups (Sokolovsky, 1985). Social workers are well-positioned to extend current knowledge on the precursors, correlates, and outcomes of these conditions and to use this information in planning, delivery, and evaluation of services that will buttress the strengths and meet the needs of an increasingly diverse aging population.

This paper will focus on conceptual and methodological considerations in conducting research on nonwhite ethnic elders. The rationale for clear, consistent terminology to define and target study populations will be presented first. Theoretical and conceptual issues, particularly as they relate to measurement for and across different racial, ethnic, and cultural groups, will then be addressed. The paper will conclude with a discussion of issues related to design, data collection, and analysis. Survey and cross-cultural methodologies, which have dominated research on ethnic aging, will be emphasized in discussions of terminology and measurement. Other methodologies will then be introduced in relation to design, data collection, and analysis.

TERMINOLOGY

Race, Ethnicity, and National Origin

Race, ethnicity and nativity are separate, equally valuable, indicators for distinguishing subgroup populations of the aged. However, lack of consistent operational definitions of these terms has led to the conflation and confusion of race and ethnicity, often to the detriment of persons studied (Zambrana, 1991). Gordon (1964, p. 27) broadly defines ethnic groups as social groups distinguished by "race, religion, or national origin." African and Native Americans are mainly distinguished by race, while religion is a central feature of ethnicity for Jews, Mormons, and Sikhs, and national origin is used to identify many European-origin groups (Gelfand, 1994). National origin is especially salient for immigrant groups, e.g., Latinos and Asian Americans, each of which has unique social, political, and cultural histories and specific migration and settlement patterns. Careful distinction of subgroups by nativity will help to guard against overgeneralization.

It is also important to assess minority (Jackson, Antonnuci, & Gibson, 1990) and social class (O'Rand, 1990) statuses. Gelfand (1994) cites Louis Wirth's (1945, p. 348) classic definition of minority as " . . . a group of people who, because of their physical or cultural characteristics, are singled out from the others in the society in which they live for differential and unequal treatment, and who therefore regard themselves as objects of collective discrimination." Although overemphasizing minority status can exaggerate its influence relative to other factors, failure to consider its current and cumulative effects risks overlooking deprivations of nonwhite ethnic elders over the life course that differentially shape their aging (Jackson, Antonnuci, & Gibson, 1995). Minority status is thus an important contextual factor to consider in selecting a research topic, designing a study, and interpreting findings in aging research (Liu, 1982). Likewise, measures of social class are needed in order to disentangle the role of sociocultural factors from minority group membership (Holzberg, 1982; O'Rand, 1990) and to ensure that study findings adequately represent low-income groups (Zambrana, 1991).

The Politics of Identification

The federal government collects race and ethnicity data to meet legislative and administrative needs such as civil rights monitoring and enforcement. Standards for these data are defined by the Office of Management and Budget's (OMB) Statistical Policy Directive No. 15, "Race and Ethnic Standards for Federal Statistics and Administrative Reporting." In response to criticism that the basic racial and ethnic categories set by the current version (in force since 1977) do not reflect the increasing racial and ethnic diversity of the population, efforts to evaluate the effects of possible changes in racial/ethnic coding were launched in 1993. Data from a May 1995 Current Population Survey (CPS) supplement to test alternative methods for collecting racial and ethnic information are now being evaluated (U.S. Department of Labor, 1995).

Because social science researchers customarily adopt the racial/ethnic coding conventions of the U.S. Bureau of the Census, coding terminology affects the collection, interpretation, and use of data. For example, researchers now routinely replace the Bureau's "black" and "Hispanic" categories with African American and Latino, respectively. These newer terms essentially define the same categories as the original ones, but they better reflect the historical, social, and cultural roots of these groups.

Moreover, new systems of classification promote the recognition and study of intra-group heterogeneity. Racial/ethnic coding of Hispanic/Latino is a good example. Hayes-Bautista and Chapa (1987) describe the social and political evolution of the "Hispanic" category, which the OMB defined in 1978 as, "A person of Mexican, Puerto Rican, Cuban, Central, or South American or other Spanish culture or origin, regardless of race" (Federal Register, 1978, p. 19269). As the authors point out, this definition mixes "a culturally derived term (Hispanic) that is operationalized partially by nationality, partially by culture, and partially not at all by the open-ended phrase ' . . . other-Spanish . . . origin' " (p. 64). Most research on Latinos has thus ignored the diverse cultural, historical, demographic and ecological conditions of Hispanic national origin groups in the United States, merging Mexican Americans, Cuban Americans, Puerto Ricans, and others into one "Hispanic" category (Aguirre & Bigelow, 1983). A two-stage alternative coding strategy of the Census Bureau first requires identification as Hispanic, Latino, or Spanish origin, then requests information on national origin.

Regardless of the system used to classify race/ethnicity, political issues will continue to influence terminology and hence research methodology. For, as Bosley (1996) points out, "official" Census categories and policies on which they are based are first and foremost political and only secondarily of scientific interest or utility. Racial/ethnic coding will continue to be based on self-identification from a predetermined, forced-choice response format, posing potential threats to conceptual clarity, measurement validity, sampling strategies, and confidence in inferences. Further, any precision gained by increasing the number of ethnic codes may in fact dilute the political presence and power of ethnic minorities vis-à-vis the white majority (Bosley, 1996). This could be problematic for the relatively small numbers of nonwhite ethnic elders.

CONCEPTUAL, THEORETICAL, AND MEASUREMENT ISSUES

Bastida (1987) cites Hempel's (1952) observation that concepts, as the building blocks of theories, denote phenomena and thereby isolate features of the world considered to be important at a given point in time. For theory building, concepts need to communicate a uniform meaning to all who use them. Establishing the relevancy and adequacy of theoretical constructs developed in research on older whites, and the equivalency of these constructs across different nonwhite ethnic groups, is thus a priority in cross-ethnic group research.

Major theories of aging in this century have focused on adjustment and adaptation in old age rather than life course development (Jackson, Antonnuci, & Gibson, 1995). Markides, Liang, and Jackson (1990) identify four main dependent variables in this literature: (1) mental health, (2) physical health, (3) intergenerational family relationships; and (4) the status of the aged in society. Arguing for a systematic appraisal of concepts in each of these domains for each group of ethnic elders, they use subjective measures of psychological well-being to illustrate the inadequacy of these indicators for assessing ethnic minority elders.

Self-evaluative judgments are made with respect to important reference groups, or those groups to which an individual orients herself or himself, regardless of actual membership (Singer, 1981). For example, self-ratings of health status are generally made with respect to others in one's age group, not to persons twenty, or even ten years younger or older. Favorable appraisals of psychological well-being by ethnic minority elders may thus reflect a judgment vis-à-vis others in their situation, although such an assessment may be incongruent with objective circumstances. Similarly, concepts like leisure and retirement may not be meaningful to the life experiences of older adults who have had to struggle to survive.

The public policy debate on intergenerational equity sparked by Preston (1984a; 1984b) in the mid-1980s illustrates the risk of overgeneralization associated with ignoring minority group status and social class. Preston and others (Lamm, 1985; Longman, 1985, 1986) argued that differential treatment of the young and the old by government programs creates different and unequal opportunities. Specifically, they linked economic costs of the generations by alleging that the young are being deprived of opportunities for well-being because of excessive allocation of resources to the old (Marshall, Cook, & Marshall, 1993).

This theory of intergenerational equity disregards ethnic minority and socioeconomic statuses on several counts. First, while overall poverty rates for the aged have fallen since the 1960s, most gains have been for whites. In 1989, 9.6% of whites aged 65 plus reported incomes below the federal poverty level, as compared to 20.6% and 30.8% of same-aged Hispanics and Blacks, respectively (U.S. Bureau of the Census, 1990). The theory also posits intergenerational competition based on unequal opportunities. Yet racism, discrimination, and poverty tend to diminish opportunities across generations of poor, ethnic minority families. Indeed, the scarcity of resources faced by these families raises another inadequacy of the theory–its failure to address the substantial informal intergenerational transfers among lower class ethnic minority families that stem from a combination of cultural norms and preferences and a need to pool resources to ensure survival (Mutran, 1985; Stack, 1974; Taylor & Chatters, 1991). This widely discussed theory of intergenerational conflict is thus based on the expectations and experiences of the white majority.

Measurement Equivalence

Establishing measurement equivalence is critical in cross-ethnic group research. Markides, Liang, and Jackson (1990) describe a hierarchy of three related types of equivalence–conceptual, metric, and structural. *Conceptual equivalence* refers to assuring that research materials and observed behaviors mean the same thing across two or more cultures. *Metric equivalence*, which assumes conceptual equivalence, means that observed indicators have the same relationships with theoretical constructs across different cultures. The third, *structural equivalence*, means that the causal linkages between a given construct and its consequences are invariant across different cultures. Structural equivalence assumes both conceptual and metric equivalence.

Standard methods of translation and validation are used to promote conceptual and linguistic equivalence in measures across groups. Bracken and Barona (1991) discuss rigorous guidelines for test translation, validation, and use in multicultural, multilingual assessment that are based on psychometric, linguistic, cultural and practical considerations. Briefly, these include a source to target translation, followed by blind back-translation, then repetition of these two steps as necessary to reduce discrepancies. Once the two forms are as close as possible, a bilingual review committee examines the translated version to ensure that it is appropriate for respondents across social, regional, and national origins. A pilot phase is next, followed by extensive field testing and item analysis to identify problems with specific items, directions, or subsample performance. Finally, appropriate norms are established (Kamphaus & Lozano, 1984). Minimal standards for assessing the technical adequacy of translated measures are subtest, scale and total test floors, ceilings, item gradients, test-re-test reliabilities, internal consistencies and validity (Werner & Campbell, 1970).

The emic-etic distinction coined by linguist Kenneth Pike (1954; 1990) may be helpful in clarifying equivalency. (Implications of this concept for data collection and analysis are addressed subsequently.) Emic refers to folk or indigenous perspectives in a culture and etic addresses a phenomenon or its characteristics that have a common, or core, meaning across cultures. Emic aspects thus differ in two cultures, but each emic is related to a shared etic core that is constructed by the analyst on the basis of cross-cultural knowledge. Description of a phenomenon for each culture thus consists of an etic core plus the culture's emic aspects.

Factor analyses and multitrait-multimethod analyses are commonly used to identify unique (emic) and shared (etic) constructs across cultures and to explore the convergent and divergent validity of constructs assessed by a given scale relative to other scales and to other theoretical constructs (Markides, Liang, & Jackson, 1990). Methodological triangulation is another useful way to establish conceptual equivalence. For example, data from qualitative methods such as in-depth case studies or focus groups may be used to inform the development of quantitative measures and/or to validate their use within and across groups.

Metric and structural equivalence are assessed mainly by factor analyzing measures for different groups, then comparing their respective factorial structures. Alwin and Jackson (1981) and Liang, Tran, and Markides (1988) describe procedures for analyzing factorial invariance across cultural groups and for using structural equation approaches to achieve valid generalizations across groups. In addition to being the preferred method for demonstrating measurement equivalence across multiple groups (Hertzog, 1987; Schaie & Hertzog, 1985), Schaie (1995, p. 572) notes that structural equation models are especially useful for aging studies because the unidirectionality of time permits better guides for specifying causal pathways than is possible in studies with single observation points only.

Minority and Social Class Considerations in Measurement

Some scholars argue that because racial minorities tend to experience a different process of development and aging in U.S. society, they should be studied within a culturally pluralistic framework that may be at odds with the measurement equivalence sought by Western modes of social science inquiry (Cardenas & Arce, 1982; Jackson, 1989a; Liu, 1982). Noting that direct translations of measures may not be culturally or linguistically appropriate for low-income minorities, Zambrana (1991) suggests an alternative strategy for translating measures with these populations. Arguing that back-translations make unwarranted assumptions about the validity of the data, she recommends that bilingual persons of the ethnic origin who are experienced in the community initially translate and review the instrument to assure correct colloquial words, symbolic meaning, and word structure.

Other sources of error in cross-ethnic group research must then be examined for low-income ethnic minorities, each with respect to participants' age. The first is careful attention to cultural, linguistic, educational and literacy level, conceptual relevance, and validity in design and presentation of the instrument (Grady & Wallston, 1988). Older adults are likely to have less formal education than members of subsequent birth cohorts, and the same holds for more recent immigrants. Second, the cross-cultural integrity of an instrument's psychometric properties with specific subgroups is established through extensive pretesting and piloting. To improve the meaningfulness and saliency of questions, modified cross-cultural procedures may be used to establish the validity of concepts and questions (Becerra & Shaw, 1984; Jackson, 1989a; Liu, 1982). Third, indigenous interviewers are trained (Tom-Orme, 1991) and matched to respondents on race (Bradburn, 1983), language (Cardenas & Arce, 1982), and, when possible, on sex (Gelfand & Yee, 1991) and perhaps educational level (Weeks & Moore, 1981).

Because social science research involves power relationships, usually between a dominant researcher and subordinate subjects, the characteristics of persons involved in research on vulnerable populations raise special ethical and political issues (Stanfield, 1993, 1994). The service needs of ethnic communities, particularly when coupled with the social vulnerability of the aged, are thus crucial considerations for persons who study nonwhite ethnic elders (Kahana & Felton, 1977). Much research on ethnic minorities has been conducted by white "outsiders," who may be better able to maintain the objectivity that is needed to develop, administer, and interpret findings from standardized study protocols. However, the advantages of an outsider perspective are often countered by reduced validity when only highly structured instruments and protocols are used to examine complex social or behavioral phenomena.

Use of indigenous interviewers can help to improve the validity and credibility of studies of low-income persons who are members of ethnic minority groups. As Aguilar (1981) observes, indigenous interviewers tend to have background knowledge of the culture, language, and local conditions and are more cognizant and accepting of the complexity of these conditions than are outsiders. They are also more effective in obtaining cooperation from the study population, as they usually have more time, comfort, and understanding. Finally, insiders to the ethnic community may lessen power differentials of status, education, or wealth between the researcher and the local culture, enhance communication and trust, and be conducive to research as a human enterprise to improve the lives of members of their ethnic group (Light & Kleiber, 1981).

SAMPLING AND RESPONSE ERRORS IN SURVEY RESEARCH

In addition to measurement-related errors, sampling error and non-response biases that are common in survey research are magnified by identification and distribution issues inherent in sampling rare populations like ethnic minorities and the aged (Jackson, 1989a; Kalton & Anderson, 1989). Sampling errors can result from both non-random sampling strategies and insufficient sample sizes for even basic within-group analyses.

With few exceptions, surveys of nonwhite ethnic elders have been limited to comparisons with same-aged whites, with the latter treated as a "normative" model or standard. Minority-majority comparisons on morbidity and mortality rates and service variables are important, but progress on improving markers of well-being and access, availability, and use of services depends on knowledge that is sensitive to the experiential and behavioral context of discrete population groups (Stanford & Yee, 1991). Even studies that oversample the ethnic aged tend to focus on only one or two groups, so that results can only be expressed dichotomously, e.g., white versus African American. This strategy further obscures the diversity among older adults and precludes development of new insights on issues that impact sub-groups differentially (Eichberg, 1991; Markides, Liang, & Jackson, 1990).

Studies of small or geographically isolated groups such as Native Americans and Asian/Pacific Islanders require special sampling designs (LaViest, 1995). Markides, Liang, and Jackson (1990) describe several alternative selection strategies, e.g., random sampling from households in high density ethnic group locales. Again, care is needed to ensure inclusion of group members that represent significant sources of variation, e.g., social class, national origin, and length of residency in the United States.

Age is another important source of variability, as "old" (65-84) and "old-old" (85+) age groups differ considerably on important dimensions of well-being and need. Studies seeking to represent the general aged population should sample the widest possible age range of elders in order to permit analyses of age differences. In addition, due to differential patterns of morbidity and mortality, age 55 may more appropriately designate the onset of old age for nonwhite ethnic groups.

Non-response biases are another source of error. Herzog and Rodgers (1982, 1988) report that older persons: (1) have higher non-response rates, especially in telephone interviews, (2) give more "don't know" responses, (3) are less productive in open-ended questions, (4) use stereotypic response styles, yielding more measurement and random error, and (5) are more susceptible to the influences of interviewer behaviors. Nonrespondents in studies of older adults tend to be more disadvantaged than respondents in many areas, including health and education (Thomas, 1989).

Far less is known about older ethnic minority populations. Resistance to being subjects in social science research due to fear and suspicion of prejudice and mistreatment, whether real or perceived, remains strong (American Psychiatric Association, 1994). Members of older age cohorts in particular may need to be educated about the purposes and expected outcomes of a project and about their role as respondents in standardized protocols (Beccera & Zambrana, 1985). Use of naturalistic methods of inquiry, either singly or in tandem with quantitative designs (Burnette, 1994; Connidis, 1983), may also help to assuage concerns about participation.

DESIGN AND PERSPECTIVE ISSUES

This section discusses two major, interrelated design issues. The first extends the above discussion of conceptual and methodological issues associated with survey research to acquiring different types of knowledge using qualitative designs. The second addresses the need for analytic models that capture the complexity of research on nonwhite ethnic elders, specifically using a life course perspective.

Qualitative Gerontology and Ethnic Aging

Knowledge of ethnic aging acquired from surveys, experiments, and other quantitative designs may be balanced and deepened by data from naturalistic or qualitative methods of inquiry (Fry & Keith, 1986; Gubrium & Sankar, 1993; Neugarten, 1985; Reinharz & Rowles, 1988). According to Reinharz and Rowles (1988, p. 6), "Qualitative studies in gerontology are concerned with describing patterns of behavior and processes of interaction as well as revealing the meanings, values, and intentionalities that pervade elderly people's experience or the experience of others in relation to old age." Efforts to understand and make sense of individual and collective human experience are a hallmark of qualitative research. Further, and in sharp contrast to the aims of objectivity and neutrality that characterize the positivist research tradition, action-oriented methods informed by critical theory regard the empowerment of participants as an intentional, integral aspect of the research process. Examples are feminist studies (Cook & Fonow, 1990), ethnic studies (Stanfield, 1994) and participative inquiry (Reason, 1994).

The three main strategies for gathering qualitative data are examining archived historical materials, in-depth interviewing, and ethnographic methods. Like standardized measures and interview protocols, qualitative designs also have conceptual, methodological, and ethical issues. The widely used "life review" originally described by Butler (1963) is used as an illustration. Butler and others (Cohler, 1982, 1991; Kaminsky, 1984; Myerhoff, 1978, 1982) have suggested that use of in-depth interviewing techniques to gather life histories or stories may yield psychological benefits for some narrators. In reviewing the literature on this methodology, Luborsky (1993) reports that its value derives from rekindling personal identity and meaning in life by reconnecting people to earlier accomplishments, fond memories, and valued identities. He attributes its broad appeal to the alleged empowerment of the narrator, whose life experiences and personal meaning are given voice in a public forum. But inasmuch as the narration is a co-construction of participants, the methodology may be problematic for gathering and analyzing life histories of nonwhite ethnic elders.

Luborsky (1993, p. 446) further observes, "In brief, the raw data of life histories are highly processed according to situational, professional, and cultural norms not controlled by the person whose life we depict." Cultural and historical forces that shape the researcher's interpretation of themes and the context and conventions for data gathering thus "constrain their value as research data or as vehicles for enhancing well-being." Here, postmodernists might argue that since all knowledge is contextual and generated dialectically, there are no "received truths" and no value-free social science. But Stanfield (1993, p. 8) takes up Luborsky's thread and applies it to issues of authority and authenticity in the research enterprise.

He contends that the personal experience focus that is so integral to qualitative research is particularly problematic in racial/ethnic research. Because Euro-Americans have exercised hegemony over the rules of procedure and evidence, even nonwhite ethnic "insiders" hew to these conventions in collecting and interpreting data. The extent to which Euro-American researchers can apprehend the inter-subjective experiences of persons of color in order to achieve an emic perspective is also unclear. Andersen (1993) quotes Blauner and Wellman (1973, p. 329) on this point:

> There are certain aspects of racial phenomena, however, that are particularly difficult, if not impossible, for a member of the oppressing group to grasp empirically and formulate conceptually. These barriers are existential and methodological as well as political and ethical.

The influence of these barriers on building knowledge and understanding of the ethnic aging experience is evidenced by the dearth of qualitative research on nonwhite older adults by ethnic scholars (ethnographic work by Burton and her colleagues [e.g., Burton & Dilworth-Anderson, 1991; Burton & Stack, 1993] on multigenerational African-American families is a notable exception). White social scientists have made important contributions to knowledge about aging among ethnic minority populations, and the racial and ethnic background of researchers need not be a litmus test for working in this area (Gibson, 1989). However, until more persons of color are brought into qualitative gerontology, the gap in "insider" knowledge will remain.

The Life Course Perspective

In 1989, the Gerontological Society of America Task Force on Minority Issues published four editorials in the *Journals of Gerontology* to promote research on ethnic minority elders. Here and elsewhere (Jackson, Antonucci, & Gibson, 1995), Jackson (1989b) and Gibson (1989) call for a research agenda in aging that employs a developmental life course rather than a late-life focus. From this perspective, age changes in individual development and adaptation are incorporated into a framework of changing social structures, and micro and macro level factors are viewed as reciprocal (Maddox & Campbell, 1985).

Ryder (1964) observed that because social change is ongoing, different cohorts grow up and grow old differently. This observation enhanced interest in the use of cohort analysis to understand behavior related to changes in age-stratified social structures and patterns of aging in successive cohorts.

According to this model, members of each cohort develop common response patterns, then each cohort, "exerts a collective force as it moves through the age-stratified society, pressing for adjustments in social roles and social values" (Riley, 1985, p. 403). The model blends two central theoretical perspectives on aging–one focuses on the consequences of variations in age structure and the other emphasizes the importance of unique cohort characteristics as a result of experiencing particular historical events (Carter, 1994). Because age, historical period, and cohort membership each have a distinctive impact on outcomes in the aging process, research using the life-course model requires consideration of all three perspectives.

Consider, for example, the acculturation of immigrants. Gelfand and Yee (1991) cite estimates by Vobedja (1990) that immigration accounted for more than one third of population growth in the United States during the 1980s, primarily due to an influx of Asian and Hispanic populations. Yet, as these authors note, very little research in gerontology has addressed this topic, and current anti-immigration fervor may further impede knowledge development. The acculturation process for immigrants differs across the life course and is affected by age, period, and cohort variables, including age at immigration, length of residency in the United States, personal, social, and political reasons for moving, fluency in English, size of ethnic community, and proximity of children and other relatives.

The personal meaning of ethnicity and age also varies at different stages of the life course (Gibson, 1989; Guttman, 1986) and in variant contexts (Luborsky & Rubinstein, 1987). Cohort effects may reflect an immigrant group's socialization to ethnic and host cultures, and period effects may capture historical changes that are especially relevant for certain groups (Markides, Liang, & Jackson, 1990). Teasing out the complex interactions of culture, social class, individual and group histories, and societal discrimination and racism and the influence of these interactions on the aging process of nonwhite ethnic elders will require multivariate and structural equation modeling (Markides & Mindel, 1987). Locating the aging experience in specific social, cultural, and subjective contexts and understanding how these contexts influence the experience of aging will require methods that are comparative, holistic, emic, and qualitative (Keith, 1990).

CONCLUSION

Research is a vital venue for building theory, influencing social policy, and informing social work practice. Conceptual and methodological tools to further current understanding of how people age within different racial, ethnic, and cultural contexts are increasingly available. This paper has discussed issues to consider when seeking out, using, and evaluating these tools in researching elderly groups of color. Clarifying terminology used to categorize sectors of the older population and acknowledging the socio-political underpinnings of ethnic coding should promote more reliable and ethical use of these classification systems.

Use of the full repertoire of quantitative and qualitative designs and analytic strategies will help to establish cross-ethnic group equivalency of measures and instruments and ensure the integrity and appropriateness of their use with different populations of older adults. The broadest range of methodologies is also needed to produce the most integrated and robust understanding of the aging process across populations. Increased availability of secondary data sources using representative samples that include or target nonwhite ethnic elders now permits fuller studies of personal and family characteristics, social, economic, and health status, and the needs and service use patterns of understudied groups of older adults. However, LaVeist (1995) reported in a recent review of federal data sets that there are enough whites and African Americans in most data sets, but insufficient numbers of Hispanics, American Indians, Alaska Natives, Asian Americans, and Pacific Islanders. Specialized sampling strategies are thus still needed to adequately assess the strengths and needs of these racial/ethnic groups and their component subgroups.

Finally, a life course perspective will promote awareness and understanding of race and ethnicity as crucial aspects of human development and aging, rather than simply as sources of error in analyses of measures taken in late life. Zambrana (1991, p. 226) nicely summarizes this mode of research: "Cross-cultural research requires not only technical skill but real-life knowledge of the experiences of non-dominant cultures, non-middle class groups, a willingness to work with community providers, and a commitment to apply the knowledge to the needs of the underserved groups . . . [in order to] generate meaningful data in the service of social change for those who have given us their knowledge, life experiences, and time."

Social work researchers will need both the technical skills and the personal and professional commitment to achieve these objectives.

REFERENCES

Aguilar, J.L. (1981). Insider research: An ethnography of a debate. In D. Messerschmidt (Ed.) *Anthropologists at home in North America: Methods and issues in the study of one's own society* (pp. 15-26). Cambridge: Cambridge University Press.

Aguirre, B.E. & Bigelow, A. (1983). The aged in Hispanic groups: A review. *International Journal of Aging and Human Development, 17* (3), 177-201.

Alwin, D.F. & Jackson, D.J. (1981). Applications of simultaneous factor analysis to issues of factorial invariance. In D.J. Jackson & E.F. Borgatta (Eds.) *Factor analysis and measurement* (pp. 249-278). London: Sage.

American Association of Retired Persons (AARP) (1995). *A profile of older Americans: 1995.* Program Resources Department, AARP and Administration Aging. Washington, DC: U.S. Department of Health and Human Services.

American Psychiatric Association (1994). *Ethnic minority elderly: A task force report of the American Psychiatric Association.* Washington, DC: Author.

Andersen, M. (1993). Studying across difference: Race, class, and gender in qualitative research. In J.H. Stanfield, II & R.M. Dennis (Eds.) *Race and ethnicity in research methods* (pp. 39-52). Newbury Park, CA: Sage.

Bastida, E. (1987). Issues of conceptual discourse in ethnic research and practice. In D.E. Gelfand & C.M. Barresi (Eds.) *Ethnic dimensions of aging* (pp. 51-63). New York: Springer.

Becerra, R.M. & Shaw, D. (1984). *The Hispanic elderly: A research reference guide.* New York: University Press of America.

Becerra, R.M. & Zambrana, R.E. (1985). Methodological approaches to research on Hispanics. *Social Work Research and Abstracts, 21* (2), 42-49.

Blauner, R. & Wellman, D. (1973). Toward the decolonization of social research. In J. Ladner (Ed.) *The death of white sociology.* New York: Vintage.

Bosley, J. (1996). "Official" race and ethnicity. <BosleyJ@ORE.PSB.BLS.GOV.> January 17, 1996.

Bracken, B.A. & Barona, A. (1991). State of the art procedures for translating, validating and using psychoeducational tests in cross-cultural assessment. *School Psychology International, 12,* 119-132.

Bradburn, N.M. (1983). Response effects. In P.H. Rossi, J.D. Wright, & A.B. Anderson (Eds.) *Handbook of survey research* (pp. 289-328). New York: Academic Press.

Burnette, D. (1994). Managing chronic illness alone in late life: Sisyphus at work. In C. Reissman (Ed.) *Qualitative studies in social work research* (pp. 5-27). Newbury Park, CA: Sage.

Burton, L.M. & Dilworth-Anderson, P. (1991). The intergenerational family roles of aged black Americans. *Marriage & Family Review, 16,* 311-330.

Burton, L.M. & Stack, C.B. (1993). Conscripting kin: Reflections on family, generation, and culture. In P.A. Cowan, D. Field, D.A. Hansen, A. Skolnick, & G.E. Swanson (Eds.) *Family, self and society: Toward a new agenda for family research* (pp. 103-113). Hillsdale, NJ: Lawrence Erlbaum Associates.

Butler, R.N. (1963). The life review: An interpretation of reminiscence in the aged. *Psychiatry, 26,* 55-76.

Cardenas, G. & Arce, C.H. (1982). The National Chicano Survey: Recruiting bilingual interviewers. In W.T. Liu (Ed.) *Methodological problems in minority research* (pp. 41-59). Chicago, IL: Pacific/Asian American Mental Health Research Center.

Carter, J. (1994). *Elderly cohort migration patterns: Methodological prescriptions for future research.* New York: Garland Publishing, Inc.

Cohler, B. (1982). Personal narrative and life course. In P. Baltes & O. Brim (Eds.) *Life-span development and behavior*, Vol. 4. New York: Academic Press.

Cohler, B. (1991). The life story and the study of resilience and response to adversity. *Journal of Narrative and Life History*, *1*, 169-200.

Connidis, I. (1983). Integrating qualitative and quantitative methods in survey research on aging: An assessment. *Qualitative Sociology*, *6* (4), 334-352.

Cook, J.A. & Fonow, M.M. (1990). Knowledge and women's interests: Issues of epistemology and methodology in feminist sociological research. In J. Nielsen (Ed.) *Feminist research methods: Exemplary reading in the social sciences* (pp. 69-93). Boulder, CO: Westview.

Eichberg, R.D. (1991). The health care of Hispanics. Letter to the editor. *Journal of the American Medical Association*, *264* (16), 2064.

Federal Register, Vol. 43, No. 87, Thursday, May 4, 1978, p. 19269.

Fry, C. & Keith, J. (1986). *New methods for old age research*. Boston: Bergin & Garvey.

Gelfand, D.E. (1994). *Aging and ethnicity*. New York: Springer.

Gelfand, D.E. & Yee, B.W.K. (1991). Influence of immigration, migration, and acculturation on the fabric of aging in America. *Generations*, *15* (4), 7-10.

Gibson, R.C. (1989). Minority aging research: Opportunity and challenge. *Journal of Gerontology: Social Sciences*, *44*, S2-S3.

Gordon, M.M. (1964). *Assimilation in American life*. New York: Oxford University Press.

Grady, K. & Wallston, B.S. (1988). *Research in health care settings*. Newbury Park, CA: Sage.

Gubrium, J. & Sankar, A. (Eds.) (1993). *Qualitative methods in aging research*. New York: Sage.

Guttman, D. (1986). A perspective on Euro-American elderly. In C. Hayes, R. Kalish, & D. Guttman (Eds.) *European-American elderly*. New York: Springer.

Hayes-Bautista, D.E. & Chapa, J. (1987). Latino terminology: Conceptual bases for standardized terminology. *American Journal of Public Health*, *77*, 61-68.

Hempel, C.G. (1952). Fundamentals of concept formation in empirical science. In *International Encyclopedia of Unified Science*, Vol. II (7). Chicago: University of Chicago Press.

Hertzog, C. (1987). Applications of structural equation models in gerontological research. In K.W. Schaie (Ed.) *Annual review of gerontology and geriatrics* (pp. 265-293),Vol. 7. New York: Springer.

Herzog, A.R. & Rodgers, W.L. (1982). *Surveys of older Americans: Some methodological investigations*. Final report to the National Institute on Aging, Institute for Social Research, The University of Michigan, Ann Arbor, MI.

Herzog, A.R. & Rodgers, W.L. (1988). Age and response rates to interview sample surveys. *Journal of Gerontology: Social Sciences*, *3* (6), S200-S205.

Holzberg, C.S. (1982). Ethnicity and aging: Anthropological perspectives on more than just the minority elderly. *The Gerontologist*, *22*, 249-257.

Jackson, J.S. (1989a). Methodological issues in survey research on older minority adults. In M.P. Lawton & A.R. Herzog (Eds.) *Special research methods for gerontology* (pp. 137-161). Amityville, NY: Baywood Publishing Co.

Jackson, J.S. (1989b). Race, ethnicity, and psychological theory and research. *Journal of Gerontology: Psychological Sciences, 44*, S1-S2.

Jackson, J.S., Antonnuci, T.C. & Gibson, R.C. (1990). Cultural, racial, and ethnic minority influences on aging. In J.E. Birren & K.W. Schaie (Eds.) *Handbook of the psychology of aging* (3rd edition) (pp. 103-123). New York: Academic Press.

Jackson, J.S. Antonnuci, T.C. & Gibson, R.C. (1995). Ethnic and cultural factors in research on aging and mental health: A life-course perspective. In D. Padgett (Ed.) *Handbook on ethnicity, aging, and mental health* (pp. 22-46). Westport, CT: Greenwood Press.

Jackson, J.J. & Ensley, D.E. (1990-91). Ethnogerontology's status and complementary and conflicting and cultural concerns for American minority elders. *Journal of Minority Aging, 12*, 41-78.

Kahana, E. & Felton, B.J. (1977). Social context and personal need: A study of Polish and Jewish aged. *Journal of Social Issues, 33* (4), 56-74.

Kalton, G. & Anderson, D.W. (1989). Sampling rare populations. In M.P. Lawton & A.R. Herzog (Eds.) *Special research methods for gerontology* (pp. 7-30). Amityville, NY: Baywood Publishing Co.

Kaminsky, M. (1994). *Uses of reminiscence: New ways of working with older adults.* New York: The Haworth Press, Inc.

Kamphaus, R.W. & Lozano, R. (1984). Developing local norms for individually administered tests. *School Psychology Review, 13*, 491-498.

Keith, J. (1990). Age in social and cultural context: Anthropological perspectives. In R. Binstock & L. George (Eds.) *Handbook on aging and the social sciences* (3rd edition) (pp. 91-111). San Diego: Academic Press.

Lamm, R.D. (1985). *Megatraumas: America in the year 2000.* Boston: Houghton Mifflin.

LaVeist, T.A. (1995). Data sources for aging research on racial and ethnic groups. *The Gerontologist, 35* (3), 328-339.

Levine, E.K. (1982). Old people are not alike: Social class, ethnicity/race, and sex are bases for important differences. In J.E. Sieber (Ed.) *The ethics of social research* (pp. 127-143). New York: Springer-Verlag.

Liang, J., Tran, T.V. & Markides, K.S. (1988). Differences in the structure of Life Satisfaction Index in three generations of Mexican Americans. *Journal of Gerontology, 43*, 1-7.

Light, L. & Kleiber, N. (1981). Interactive research in a feminist setting: The Vancouver women's health collective. In D.A. Messerschmidt (Ed.) *Anthropologists at home in North America: Methods and issues in the study of one's own society* (pp. 167-182). Cambridge: Cambridge University Press.

Liu, W.T. (Ed.) (1982). Introduction. *Methodological problems in minority research* (pp. 1-9). Occasional Paper No. 7. Chicago, IL: Pacific/Asian American Mental Health Research Center.

Longman, P. (1985, June). Justice between generations. *Atlantic Monthly*, pp. 73-81.

Longman, P. (1987). Age wars: The coming battle between young and old. *Futurist, 29* (1), 8-11.

Luborsky, M.R. (1993). The romance with personal meaning in gerontology: Cultural aspects of life themes. *The Gerontologist, 33* (4), 445-452.

Luborsky, M.R. & Rubinstein, R. (1987). Ethnicity and lifetimes: Self-concepts and situational contexts of ethnic identity in late life. In D. Gelfand & C.M. Barresi (Eds.) *Ethnic dimensions of aging* (pp. 18-34). New York: Springer Publishing Co.

Maddox, G.L. & Campbell, R.T. (1985). Scope, concepts, and methods in the study of aging. In R.H. Binstock & E. Shanas (Eds.) *Handbook of aging and the social sciences* (2nd edition) (pp. 3-31). New York: Van Nostrand-Reinhold.

Markides, K.S. & Mindel, C.H. (1987). *Aging and ethnicity.* Newbury Park, CA: Sage.

Markides, K.S., Liang, J. & Jackson, J.S. (1990). Race, ethnicity, and aging: Conceptual and methodological issues. In R. Binstock & L. George (Eds.) *Handbook on aging and the social sciences* (3rd edition) (pp. 112-129). San Diego: Academic Press.

Marshall, V.W., Cook, F.L. & Marshall, J.G. (1993). Conflict over intergenerational equity: Rhetoric and reality in a comparative context. In V.L. Bengtson & W.A. Achenbaum (Eds.) *The changing contract across generations* (pp. 119-140). New York: Aldine de Gruyter.

Mutran, E. (1985). Intergenerational family support among blacks and whites: Response to culture or to socio-economic differences. *Journal of Gerontology, 40*, S382-S389.

Myerhoff, B. (1979). *Number our days.* New York: Dutton.

Myerhoff, B. (1982). Life history among the elderly: Performance, visibility, and remembering. In J. Ruby (Ed.) *A crack in the mirror: Reflexive perspectives in anthropology.* Philadelphia: University of Pennsylvania.

Neugarten, B.L. (1985). Interpretive social science and research on aging. In A. Rossi (Ed.) *Gender and the life course* (pp. 291-300). New York: Aldine.

O'Rand, A.M. (1990). Stratification and the life course. In R.H. Binstock & L.K. George (Eds.) *Handbook of aging and the social sciences* (3rd edition) (pp. 130-150). New York: Academic Press.

Padgett, D. (Ed.) (1995). *Handbook on ethnicity, aging, and mental health.* Westport, CT: Greenwood Press.

Pike, K.L. (1954). *Language in relation to a unified theory of the structure of human behavior.* Part I: preliminary edition. Santa Ana, CA: Summer Institute of Linguistics.

Pike, K.L. (1990). On the emics and etics of Pike and Harris. In T.N. Headland, K.L. Pike & M. Harris (Eds.) *Emics and etics: The insider/outsider debate* (pp. 28-47). Newbury Park, CA: Sage.

Preston, S.H. (1984a). Children and the elderly: Divergent paths for America's dependents. *Demography, 21*, 435-457.

Preston, S.H. (1984b). Children and the elderly in the United States. *Scientific American, 251* (6), 44-49.

Reason, P. (1994). Three approaches to participative inquiry. In N.K. Denzin & Y.S. Lincoln (Eds.) *Handbook of qualitative research* (pp. 324-339). Thousand Oaks, CA: Sage.

Reinharz, S. & Rowles, G.D. (1988). *Qualitative gerontology.* New York: Springer.

Riley, M.W. (1985). Age strata in social systems. In R.H. Binstock & E. Shanas (Eds.) *Handbook of aging and the social sciences* (2nd edition, pp. 369-403). New York: Van Nostrand-Reinhold.

Ryder, N.B. (1965). The cohort as a concept in the study of social change. *American Sociological Review, 30,* 843-861.

Schaie, K.W. (1995). Research methods in gerontology. In G. Maddox (Editor-in-Chief) *Encyclopedia of Aging* (2nd Edition) (pp. 570-573). New York: Springer.

Schaie, K.W. & Hertzog, C. (1985). Measurement in the psychology of adulthood and aging. In J.W. Birren & K.W. Schaie (Eds.) *Handbook of the psychology of aging,* (2nd edition) (pp. 61-92). New York: Van Nostrand Reinhold.

Singer, E. (1981). Reference groups and social evaluations. In M. Rosenberg & R.H. Turner (Eds.) *Social psychology: Sociological perspectives* (pp. 66-93). New York: Basic Books.

Sokolovsky, J. (1985). Ethnicity, culture, and aging: Do differences really make a difference? *The Journal of Applied Gerontology, 4,* 6-17.

Stack, C.B. (1974). *All of kin: Strategies for survival in a black community.* New York: Harper & Row.

Stanfield, J.H., Jr. (1993). *Race and ethnicity in research methods.* Newbury Park, CA: Sage.

Stanfield, J.H., Jr. (1994). In N.K. Denzin & Y.S. Lincoln (Eds.) *Handbook of qualitative research* (pp. 175-188). Thousand Oaks, CA: Sage.

Stanford, P. & Yee, D.L. (1991). Gerontology and relevance of diversity. *Generations,* Fall/Winter, 11-14.

Taueber, C. (1990). Diversity: The dramatic reality. In S.A. Bass, E.A. Kutza, & F.M. Torres-Gil (Eds.) *Diversity in aging* (pp. 1-45). Glenville, IL: Scott, Foresman.

Taylor, R. & Chatters, L. (1991). Extended family networks of older black adults. *Journal of Gerontology, 46,* S210-S217.

Thomas, C. (1989). The effects of nonresponse and attrition on samples of elderly people. In F.J. Fowler, Jr. (Ed.) *Health Survey Research Methods.* National Center for Health Services Research. (PHS Pub. No. 89-3447). Washington, DC: United States Department of Health Services Research.

Tom-Orme, L. (1991). The search for insider-outsider partnerships in research. In *Primary Care Research: Theory and Methods,* PHS Pub. No. 91-0011, Rockville, MD: U.S. Department of Health and Human Services.

U.S. Bureau of the Census (1990). Unpublished data. *Current Population Reports* (March, 1990). Washington, DC.

U.S. Bureau of Labor Statistics (October, 1995). *A CPS Supplement for testing methods of collecting racial and ethnic information: May 1995.* USDL Pub. No. 95-428. Washington, DC: U.S. Department of Labor.

Usui, W.M. (1989). Challenges in the development of ethnogerontology. *Gerontologist, 29,* 566-568.

Vobedja, B. (1990). U.S. growth in 1980s fueled by immigrants. *Washington Post,* December 31, p. 4.

Weeks, M.G. & Moore, R.P. (1981). Ethnicity-of-interviewer effects on ethnic respondents. *Public Opinion Quarterly, 45,* 245-259.

Werner, O. & Campbell, D.T. (1970). Translating, working through interpreters, and the problem of decentering. In R. Naroll & R. Cohen (Eds.) *A handbook of method in cultural anthropology* (pp. 398-420). New York: The Natural History Press.

Wirth, L. (1945). The problem of minority groups. In R. Linton (Ed.) *The science of man in the world crisis.* New York: Columbia University Press.

Zambrana, R.E. (1991). Cross-cultural methodological strategies in the study of low income racial ethnic populations. In M.L. Grady (Ed.) *Primary care research: Theory and methods* (pp. 221-227). Rockville, MD: U.S. Department of Health and Human Services.

Application of Rasch Analysis: Exploring Differences in Depression Between African-American and White Children

Yosikazu DeRoos
Paula Allen-Meares

EDITORS' NOTE. This article presents a relatively unknown psychometric technique, Rasch analysis. In this method, data are fit to an invariant statistical model which defines a unidimensional variable; the rank ordering of items that operationalize that variable is indicative of the degree of intensity of the property being measured. The authors empirically test the supposition, which is also echoed elsewhere in this volume, that emotions such as depression are manifested differently by members of different ethnic groups. Rasch analysis, as described, can clearly be used to analyze scale data in cross-cultural comparative studies. Its potential in this regard is intriguing. However, the present study must be viewed as exploratory and suggestive only, due to its use of nonrepresentative samples and lack of control for confounding variables. The study suggests several avenues for future research: (1) Rasch analysis needs to be compared to other psychometric techniques to determine its relative advantages and disadvan-

Yosikazu DeRoos is affiliated with the Department of Social Work, New Mexico State University, P.O. Box 30001, Department 3SW, Las Cruces, NM 88003-8001. Paula Allen-Meares is affiliated with the School of Social Work, The University of Michigan, 1065 Freize Building, Ann Arbor, MI 48109-1285.

[Haworth co-indexing entry note]: "Application of Rasch Analysis: Exploring Differences in Depression Between African-American and White Children." DeRoos, Yosikazu, and Paula Allen-Meares. Co-published simultaneously in *Journal of Social Service Research* (The Haworth Press, Inc.) Vol. 23, No. 3/4, 1998, pp. 93-107; and: *Social Work Research with Minority and Oppressed Populations: Methodological Issues and Innovations* (ed: Miriam Potocky, and Antoinette Y. Rodgers-Farmer) The Haworth Press, Inc., 1998, pp. 93-107. Single or multiple copies of this article are available for a fee from The Haworth Document Delivery Service [1-800-342-9678, 9:00 a.m. - 5:00 p.m. (EST). E-mail address: getinfo@haworth.com].

tages. (2) The technique needs to be applied with random samples to ensure that differences in rank ordering of items across racial groups are not due to sampling error. (3) In a similar vein, confounding variables need to be controlled to ensure that differences are indeed attributable to ethnicity rather than some other correlated variable(s). (4) Finally, research needs to address similarities as well as differences across groups in their experience of affective states. As the authors note, we need to establish that we are measuring the same construct, even though it may be operationalized differently by each group.

SUMMARY. The use of Rasch analysis to elicit the structure of depression was investigated. Responses from 102 African-American and white adolescents were evaluated using Rasch analysis. Responses from African-Americans and whites were compared to discern differences in the operational definition of depression for the two groups. How Rasch analysis can be used to increase the understanding of depression for African-Americans and other minority groups is discussed. *[Article copies available for a fee from The Haworth Document Delivery Service: 1-800-342-9678. E-mail address: getinfo@haworth.com]*

We understand better than before that ethnicity plays a role in the way in which psychosocial disorders are manifested. We know, for example, that characteristics of depression are different for different cultural groups. Kleinman and Good (1985) write, "Cross-cultural research offers evidence of cultural variations in depressive mood, symptoms, and illness . . . " (p. 3). That depression may vary in this way has often been considered troublesome, causing some to downplay such differences and focus on those characteristics that are common among groups (Beiser, 1985). However, to do so ignores the real differences in depression that exist among different groups. Because research on a topic such as depression tends to reflect the characteristics of groups that numerically dominate the samples being studied, those characteristics associated with minority groups such as African-Americans are sometimes treated as atypical and as less important for characterizing the disorder than those that typify numerical majority groups. This may make it less likely for groups which are numerically in the minority to have their particular form of depression validated as depression. A possible consequence may be that when ethnic minority members seek help for depression, it may be more likely that the severity of the depression will be incorrectly assessed and that the depression will be characterized as atypical (Fellin, 1989).

Thus, there are two tasks for those interested in depression and ethnicity. One task is to show in a rigorous way how a disorder such as depression actually manifests itself among the various groups. The second task is to argue for the validity of the disorder in its different manifestations among the various ethnic groups.

The latter task is primarily a conceptual one. One must show that the concept of depression has coherence in its various forms, that is, that it is depression we are assessing even though it manifests itself somewhat differently among different groups. The first task is empirical. It requires a procedure that effectively delineates depression in a way characteristic for particular ethnic groups. Such a procedure must be able to identify the characteristics of depression that are typical for a particular ethnic group and to delineate those characteristics in such a way that they form an operational definition of depression for that group. This study focuses on this task. Such a procedure to rigorously delineate variables exists. It is called Rasch analysis. Rasch analysis will be discussed in more detail below.

Research about the characteristics of depression among African-Americans pertains primarily to adults. Many studies exist about childhood depression. Far fewer studies exist about the association of depression with race (Peterson et al., 1993; Dornbusch et al., 1991). Although one ought not generalize from adults to adolescents without empirical support (and this study is designed to advance that task), there is a conceptual link between the two. This is attested to by the fact that the Beck Depression Inventory is used as the base on which the Children's Depression Inventory (CDI) is built (Kovacs, 1983).

Some characteristics one might expect to find associated with the African-American experience of depression include loss of friends and support (Fellin, 1989), low self-perceptions (Bazargan & Hamm-Baugh, 1995), low self-esteem (Munford, 1994), and for a child, living in a household without the mother (Fitzpatrick, 1993). Another factor related to the African-American experience of depression is adopting a "mask of survival" and thus hiding true feelings from others. Thus, affective symptoms typical of whites may be absent from the manifestations of African-American depression (Quesada, Spears, & Ramos, 1978). Whereas suicide is not uncommon among whites who are depressed, it is less common for African-Americans. However, rather than the internally directed violence of suicide, it is more common to find violent behavior being directed toward others (Thomas & Lindenthal, 1975).

THE RASCH MEASUREMENT MODEL

The Rasch model is a normative model for constructing interval-level unidimensionality of data on a group of subjects for a set of items they have completed. The placement of items on a line that indicates greater and lesser amounts of the variable being measured constitutes operationalization of the variable. The Rasch model defines the ideal delineation of items that would constitute an objective, interval-level measuring instrument (DeRoos & Allen-Meares, 1992). In this model, measurements of characteristics of subjects and calibrations of item difficulties are conceived as probabilistic. Wright and Masters (1982) write:

> The uncertainties of experience are handled by expressing the model of how person and item parameters combine to produce observable events as a probability. In formulating the connection between idea and experience we do not attempt to specify exactly what will happen. Instead, we specify the probability of an indicative event occurring. This leaves room for the uncertainty of experience without abandoning the construction of order.

Thus, with the Rasch model, a person with more of a characteristic will always have a higher *probability* of endorsing or succeeding on an item used to measure that characteristic than a person with a lesser amount of the characteristic, regardless of the item being used to measure it. Also in the Rasch model, an item that may be more difficult to respond to affirmatively or to get right will *always* have a lower probability of being endorsed or of being successful on than a less difficult item, regardless of a person's level of the characteristic being measured by the items (Wright & Masters, 1982). Thus, the Rasch model takes into account both the trait being measured and the qualities of the items used to measure it.

> Person abilities and item difficulties are designated in logits or log odds units: A person's ability in logits is their natural log odds for succeeding on items of the kind chosen to define the "zero" point on the scale. And an item's difficulty in logits is its natural log odds for eliciting failure from persons with "zero" ability. (Wright & Stone, 1979)

With the Rasch model, person ability β and item calibration δ are combined by forming their difference: $\beta - \delta$ (Wright & Stone, 1979). This difference is the probability a person of a given ability will endorse an item of a given difficulty. Although either parameter can vary from minus to plus infinity, to keep the probability between 0 and 1, $\beta - \delta$ is applied as the exponent of a base: $\exp(\beta - \delta)$. This term is then used in the ratio: $\exp(\beta - \delta)/[1 + \exp(\beta - \delta)]$. This represents the item-characteristic curve for the Rasch model and is the Rasch probability for a person endorsing an item (Wright & Stone, 1979).

For dichotomous items, the Rasch model is:

$$\Phi_{nil} = \frac{\exp(\beta_n - \delta_{il})}{1 + \exp(\beta_n - \delta_{il})}$$

where $\emptyset_{nil}$ is the probability of person n endorsing or getting item I correct, and thus scoring 1 rather than 0 (Wright & Stone, 1979).

For items with ordered response categories such as items from the CDI, an additional parameter is added to the model. This allows the model to account for the additional steps (in CDI's case, an additional step), introduced by incrementally more difficult item categories beyond the two categories found in dichotomous items (Wright & Masters, 1982). The Rasch model for ordered response categories is (Wright & Masters, 1982):

$$\Phi_{nik} = \frac{\exp[\beta_n - (\delta_i + \tau_k)]}{1 + \exp[\beta_n - (\delta_i + \tau_k)]} \qquad k = 1, 2, \ldots, m$$

where k is the number of steps taken or thresholds successfully crossed and τ_k, the threshold parameter, is the location of the kth step in each item relative to that item's scale value (Wright & Masters, 1982).

The Rasch statistical model is *invariant*. The Rasch statistical model *defines* unidimensionality. This is often misunderstood. Often, the task is to fit a model to a body of data. In doing so, one is able to describe the data by how one has fitted a model. In Rasch analysis, the process is to determine how closely the data fit the Rasch model. This makes sense if one intends to define a variable since the Rasch model defines how a variable ought to ideally look. Thus, defining a variable requires lineariz-ing the data and calibrating the items that go into defining the variable. Since the Rasch model serves as the standard against which the data are compared, one can determine how closely one's data approximate this ideal linear standard.

Thus, to study ethnic groups, for example, one can determine which characteristics of depression are typical for the various ethnic groups and order the characteristics so that one can define which characteristics indi-cate greater or lesser degrees of severity of the disorder for that ethnic group. By doing so, one can portray depression in its most typical form for each ethnic group and validate that portrayal in an empirically rigorous way. For our paper, we take a sample of African-American and white subjects to illustrate how the disorder may manifest itself within ethnic groups and illustrate the differences that arise between such groups.

In discussing an issue such as cultural variation in the operationalization of a variable, an objection is that such variations suggest alternative construct definitions, which is seen as undesirable (Choe, 1995). However, we argue otherwise. A construct such as depression is a theoretical formulation of a variable that must be supported empirically to be considered valid. It is possible to argue that for a variable such as depression, there may be several operationalizations of the variable using the same set of items. In other words, it is possible to have a set of items that operationally defines a variable and have different item orderings that constitute the operationalization of the variable. Such differential item functioning need not be considered a problem as long as we do not require that item order be absolute. By allowing for different item orderings, we acknowledge that variables do not function independently of other variables. When the other variable is *culture*, the potential for that variable and a psychosocial variable such as depression being associated is great.

This study looks at whether there are discernable differences in the way African-American and white students operationally delineate depression. Differences should arise through the differential ordering of items along the variable line operationalized by the items of the Children's Depression Inventory.

METHOD

Instrument

The Children's Depression Inventory (CDI) is a revision and downward extension of the Beck Depression Inventory and is designed for children aged 8 to 17 (Kovacs, 1983, 1985). The CDI has 27 items, each consisting of three categories listed in order of symptom severity. The original scoring procedure dictates that all items in the scale be weighted equally and thus computing scores and determining the level of depression measured by the instrument is a simple summing of values of the categories for the items. With Rasch analysis, we are able to discern if different items measure different levels of depression and to perform measurements taking into consideration such differences.

Computer Program

Rasch analysis of the CDI was performed using BigSteps (Wright & Linacre, 1993). BigSteps is an extension of the unconditional maximum likelihood procedure developed by Wright and Panchapakesan (1969) and investigated by Wright and Douglas (1977; 1981). (For the mathematical foundation of Rasch analysis, including computational procedures and examples for computing person measures and item calibrations, the reader is directed to Wright and Masters [1982].)

Subjects

One hundred two elementary and junior high students acted as subjects of the study. Two groups of students were included, those with behavioral problems and those without. The students with behavioral problems had been identified as eligible for special education using criteria set forth in Public Law 94-142 and the students' resident state's special education guidelines. The nonhandicapped students attended the same schools as the behaviorally disordered students. The students were required to show a full scale IQ of 70 or higher. Data for the two groups were pooled.

RESULTS

The results supported our hypothesis that different operationalizations of depression would develop for African-Americans and whites. The outcomes for the two groups differ in two ways. First, the order of items that operationalize depression is different for the two groups. Second, the centrality or usefulness of some items toward the operational definition differs for the two groups. The results show that there are both similarities and differences in how depression is operationalized for African-Americans and whites.

In Figure 1, depression is depicted as it is operationalized through Rasch analysis. The item order differs between African-Americans and whites. This supports the assumption that cultural differences are associated with how depression manifests itself.

The item ordering for African-Americans begins with item # 06 of the CDI. That item, as do all items in the inventory, has three options. This item, selected as the one lowest on the metric, is *I think about bad things happening to me once in a while/I worry that bad things will happen to me/I am sure that terrible things will happen to me.* The three options specify ordered degrees of severity. The significance of the item being lowest on the metric is that such an item is useful for distinguishing between the existence or nonexistence of low levels of depression. Such an item would not be used to detect severe levels of depression.

FIGURE 1. Operational Definitions of Depression for African-American and White Subjects.

AFRICAN-AMERICAN   WHITE

AFRICAN-AMERICAN		WHITE
ITEM 25	SEVERE	ITEM 03
ITEM 07	DEPRESSION	ITEM 01
ITEM 10		ITEM 08
ITEM 03		ITEM 12
ITEM 08		ITEM 25
ITEM 22		ITEM 07
ITEM 21		ITEM 22
ITEM 05		ITEM 05
ITEM 16		ITEM 10
ITEM 23		ITEM 27
ITEM 01		ITEM 09
ITEM 02		ITEM 20
ITEM 12		ITEM 18
ITEM 11		ITEM 26
ITEM 18		ITEM 19
ITEM 26		ITEM 14
ITEM 14		ITEM 23
ITEM 24		ITEM 16
ITEM 13		ITEM 04
ITEM 20		ITEM 21
ITEM 27		ITEM 11
ITEM 09		ITEM 24
ITEM 15		ITEM 06
ITEM 17		ITEM 02
ITEM 04		ITEM 17
ITEM 19	MILD OR	ITEM 13
ITEM 06	NO DEPRESSION	ITEM 15

Note. The upper end (items 25 and 03) lists items that are useful for distinguishing more severe depression for each group. The lower end lists items that are useful for distinguishing less severe depression.

At the other end of the variable line is item # 25, which reads *I am sure somebody loves me/I am not sure if anybody loves me/Nobody really loves me.* Given its placement on the variable line, it indicates that this item can be used to distinguish between the existence or nonexistence of more severe levels of depression.

For African-Americans some of the items at the upper end of the variable line, the region that is useful for distinguishing degrees of more severe depression, are as follows:

1. #25 *I am sure somebody loves me/I am not sure if anybody loves me/Nobody really loves me.*
2. #07 *I like myself/I do not like myself/I hate myself.*
3. #10 *I feel like crying once in a while/I feel like crying many days/I feel like crying everyday.*

Characterizations of self-hate, a feeling of not being loved by another and feelings of wanting to cry everyday are reflective of symptoms of severe depression, according to the analysis.

For whites the three items at the top of the metric, indicating that these items detect severe levels of depression, are:

1. #03 *I do most things o.k./I do many things wrong/I do everything wrong.*
2. #01 *I am sad once in a while/I am sad many times/I am sad all the time.*
3. #08 *Bad things are usually not my fault/Many bad things are my fault/All bad things are my fault.*

For whites, doing everything wrong and all things being one's fault are similar in character and center on notions of self-blame, of one being faultworthy. The other item indicates what is a typical characteristic of depression among many groups, that of sadness. Chronic sadness is indicative of severe depression for whites, according to the analysis. There is no overlap in these items for African-Americans and whites. This is part of the difference to be found between the two groups.

At the other end of the variable line, the end at which items can detect mild levels of depression, are three more items. For African-Americans the three items are:

1. #06 *I think about bad things happening to me once in a while/I worry that bad things will happen to me/I am sure that terrible things will happen to me.*
2. #19 *I do not worry about aches and pains/I worry about aches and pains many times/I worry about aches and pains all the time.*
3. #04 *I have fun in many things/I have fun in some things/Nothing is fun at all.*

These items, even of the most severe options, would usually be interpreted as items that may be useful for detecting lower levels of depression or maybe for discerning other phenomena. Item # 06 sounds like an item that measures anxiety as well as depression. What these items may indicate is the difficulty in developing items that measure low levels of depression. At those levels, it may be difficult to separate those characteristics that are indicative of depression from those that are related to other phenomena. When depression becomes more severe, symptoms characteristic of depression become more pronounced and thus are easier to operationalize and therefore detect.

For whites the three items at the low end of the variable line are:

1. #15 *Doing schoolwork is not a big problem/I have to push myself many times to do my schoolwork/I have to push myself all the time to do my schoolwork.*

2. #13 *I make up my mind about things easily/It is hard to make up my mind about things/I cannot make up my mind about things.*

3. #17 *I am tired once in a while/I am tired many days/I am tired all the time.*

Here, we would make the same argument as for the previous items, that the items may be characteristic of low levels of depression but may also be indicative of something else. Having to push oneself to do schoolwork or not being able to make up one's mind may be indicative of depression but may be related to other concerns including lack of interest in schoolwork, having too much schoolwork, having competing claims on one's time, and so on.

Again, there is no overlap in the items between the two groups. That a given item is not at exactly the same location on the variable line for the two groups is not particularly significant. Slight variations in the item ordering might result in none of the items being ordered at the same point along the metric for the two groups. What is important is that items that define the ends of the metric differ. We will say more about this as we discuss the data.

Another difference is that some items clearly differ in their location in the two delineations of the variable. For example, item # 19 (see above), was calibrated by African-Americans as useful for measuring low levels of depression and by whites as a moderate level item (see Figure 1). There are several such items that distinguish the two groups. In some cases the items were ranked lower on the metric for African-Americans than for whites. Here are several:

1. #09 *I do not think about killing myself/I think about killing myself but I would not do it/I want to kill myself.*

2. #27 *I get along with people/I get into fights many times/I get into fights all the time.*

3. #12 *I like being with people/I do not like being with people many times/I do not want to be with people at all.*

In other cases, the items were ranked lower on the metric for whites than for African-Americans:

1. #21 *I have fun at school many times/I have fun at school only once in a while/I never have fun at school.*

2. #02 *Things will work out for me o.k./I am not sure if things will work out for me/Nothing will ever work out for me.*

The second, related issue is of the usefulness of items in delineating the variable. There are some items that clearly "fit" as part of the larger delineation of the variable while other items do so less effectively. If one has selected items that are conceptually appropriate, the reason some items fit better than others is usually related to the degree of association of items to other variables. While we understand that all items that define a variable correlate with other variables, some do so more than others. If an item's association with other variables is too great, it loses its usefulness as an item for clearly defining some point on a variable line. In other instances, items may have extremely low association. This, too, is a problem. In the psychosocial sphere, an item or a variable that is not associated with other variables is worthless for research.

In the CDI, there are items that work more or less effectively. This is determined by several statistics called fit statistics that determine degrees of fit of an item to the overall delineation of items. For a measuring instrument to work, the items that comprise the instrument must work together. If an item does not fit the overall delineation of the variable line, its usefulness is compromised. In Figure 2, the items are listed by their order in the CDI. Their locations relative to the single vertical line are an indication of the items' usefulness in operationalizing depression; the closer an item to the line, the more useful it is because it fits with the overall delineation of the variable.

For African-Americans, item # 3, *I do most things o.k./I do many things wrong/I do everything wrong* and item # 17, *I am tired once in a while/I am tired many days/I am tired all the time* do not fit well into the variable line. For whites, item # 5, *I am bad once in a while/I am bad many times/I am*

FIGURE 2. Usefulness of Item in the Operational Definitions of Depression for African-American and White Subjects.

AFRICAN-AMERICAN			WHITE		
01			01		
	02		02		
		03	03		
04			04		
	05				05
06			06		
07			07		
08			08		
09			09		
10				10	
11				11	
	12		12		
13			13		
14			14		
	15				15
16				16	
		17	17		
	18		18		
	19			19	
20			20		
21					21
22			22		
	23				23
24			24		
25				25	
26			26		
27			27		

MORE ‹- - - - -› LESS   MORE ‹- - - - -› LESS
USEFUL   USEFUL   USEFUL   USEFUL

Note. The distance from the line indicates degrees of usefulness, the closer to the line the more useful the item is in defining depression. Usefulness is determined by fit statistics that indicate the degree to which items fit the overall delineation of items on the variable line.

bad all the time, item # 15, *Doing schoolwork is not a big problem/I have to push myself many times to do my schoolwork/I have to push myself all the time to do my schoolwork,* item # 21, *I have fun at school many times/I have fun at school only once in a while/I never have fun at school* and item # 23, *My schoolwork is alright/My schoolwork is not as good as before/I do badly in subjects I used to be good in,* all do not work as well as the other items. For whites, three of the items above deal with school.

DISCUSSION

The analysis yielded different operational definitions of depression. A question that one asks at this point is whether the operational definition fits what we understand about depression among African-Americans. It appears it does. As noted earlier, loss of friendship and support is associated with depression. Item # 25 has as its third category *Nobody really loves me.* For an African-American adolescent, the belief that no one loves her or him, that he or she is alone, is easily understood in relation to depression. Another item, # 07 has as its upper category *I hate myself.* That item, too, is easy to understand in its relation to depression. Low self-perceptions, low self-esteem and even self-hatred, reinforced by social forces over which an adolescent may feel little control, can easily lead to depression. Both of these items are at the upper end of the variable line. In other words, if the two comments above are endorsed by an African-American adolescent, that would indicate a high level of depression. The more such items at the upper end of the variable line are endorsed, the more certain it is that a high level of depression is present.

For whites, in addition to item # 01, *I am sad all the time,* which we would regard as typically indicative of higher levels of depression, are two items, # 03 and # 08, both of which deal with self-blame, of one being faultworthy: *I do everything wrong* and *All bad things are my fault.* Although these items also ranked high for African-Americans, they did not appear at the top of the variable line for them.

This is instructive in helping us develop ways of evaluating symptoms associated with depression and to put those on a metric that can more clearly define its severity. Whereas today instruments such as the CDI give equal weight to all items, Rasch analysis allows us to recognize that the operationalization of depression, even when using the same items, may differ for different groups. In being able to develop such a metric for different groups such as African-Americans, whites and others, one can more effectively assess depression.

This study is another step in addressing the culture-specific characteristics of depression. This is a step in the direction of giving recognition to those cultural factors within which we are all embedded and of helping us to understand how culture, society and individual characteristics interact when we assess psychosocial variables such as depression.

The results from this study, given its convenience sample of African-Americans and whites, are not generalizable to larger populations. Taking larger, representative samples will help us clarify a variable such as depression for the two groups. The next step is to collect data from the two populations and to once again Rasch analyze the data. The goal is to develop culture-specific instruments which are appropriate for measuring depression within the African-American and within the white populations. We believe that Rasch analysis is one effective tool for doing exactly that.

REFERENCES

Bazargan, M., & Hamm-Baugh, V. P. (1995). The relationship between chronic illness and depression in a community of urban Black elderly persons. *Journal of Gerontology, 50*(2), 119-127.

Beiser, M. (1985). A study of depression among traditional Africans, urban North Americans, and Southeast Asian refugees. In A. Kleinman & B. Good (Eds.), *Culture and depression: Studies in the anthropology and cross-cultural psychiatry of affect and disorder* (pp. 272-298). Berkeley and Los Angeles, CA: University of California Press.

Choe, I. (1995). Learning from construct definitions. *Rasch Measurement Transactions, 9*, 439-440.

DeRoos, Y. S., & Allen-Meares, P. (1992). Rasch analysis: Its description and use analyzing the Children's Depression Inventory. *Journal of Social Service Research, 16*(3/4), 1-17.

Dornbusch, S. M., Mont-Reynand, R., Ritter, P. L., Chen, Z., & Steinberg, L. (1991). Stressful events and their correlates among adolescents of diverse backgrounds. In M. E. Colton & S. Gore (Eds.), *Adolescent stress: Causes and consequences* (pp. 111-130). New York: Aldine de Gruyter.

Fellin, P. (1989). Perspectives on depression among Black Americans. *Health and Social Work, 14*, 245-252.

Fitzpatrick, K. M. (1993). Exposure to violence and presence of depression among low-income African-American youth. *Journal of Consulting and Clinical Psychology, 61*, 528-531.

Kleinman, A., & Good, B. (Eds.). (1985). *Culture and depression: Studies in the anthropology and cross-cultural psychiatry of affect and disorder.* Berkeley and Los Angeles: University of California Press.

Kovacs, M. (1983). *The Children's Depression Inventory: A self-rated depression scale for school-aged youngsters.* Unpublished manuscript, University of Pittsburgh School of Medicine.

Kovacs, M. (1985). The Children's Depression Inventory (CDI). *Psychopharmacology Bulletin, 21,* 995-998.

Munford, M. B. (1994). Relationship of gender, self-esteem, social class, and racial identity to depression in Blacks. *Journal of Black Psychology, 20,* 157-174.

Petersen, A. C., Compas, B. E., Brooks-Gunn, J., Stemmler, M., Ey, S., & Grant, K. E. (1993). Depression in adolescence. *American Psychologist, 48,* 155-168.

Quesada, G. M., Spears, W., & Ramos, P. (1978). Interracial depressive epidemiology in the Southwest. *Journal of Health and Social Behavior, 19,* 77-85.

Thomas, C. S., & Lindenthal, J. J. (1975). The depression of the oppressed. *Mental Hygiene, 59,* 12-14.

Wright, B. D., & Douglas, G. A. (1977). Conditional versus unconditional procedures for sample-free item analysis. *Educational and Psychological Measurement, 37,* 47-60.

Wright, B. D., & Douglas, G. A. (1981). The essential process in a family of measurement models. *Psychometrika, 49,* 529-544.

Wright, B. D., & Linacre, J. M. (1993). BigSteps (Version 2.45) [Computer software]. Chicago: MESA Press.

Wright, B. D., & Panchapakesan, N. (1969). A procedure for sample-free item analysis. *Educational and Psychological Measurement, 29,* 23-37.

Wright, B. D., & Masters, G. N. (1982). *Rating scale analysis.* Chicago: MESA Press.

Wright, B. D., & Stone, M. H. (1979). *Best test design.* Chicago: MESA Press.

Index

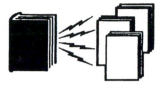

Haworth
DOCUMENT DELIVERY
SERVICE

This valuable service provides a single-article order form for any article from a Haworth journal.

- *Time Saving:* No running around from library to library to find a specific article.
- *Cost Effective:* All costs are kept down to a minimum.
- *Fast Delivery:* Choose from several options, including same-day FAX.
- *No Copyright Hassles:* You will be supplied by the original publisher.
- *Easy Payment:* Choose from several easy payment methods.

Open Accounts Welcome for . . .
- Library Interlibrary Loan Departments
- Library Network/Consortia Wishing to Provide Single-Article Services
- Indexing/Abstracting Services with Single Article Provision Services
- Document Provision Brokers and Freelance Information Service Providers

---

MAIL or *FAX* THIS ENTIRE ORDER FORM TO:

Haworth Document Delivery Service
The Haworth Press, Inc.
10 Alice Street
Binghamton, NY 13904-1580

or FAX: 1-800-895-0582
or CALL: 1-800-342-9678
9am-5pm EST

PLEASE SEND ME PHOTOCOPIES OF THE FOLLOWING SINGLE ARTICLES:
1) Journal Title: _____
    Vol/Issue/Year: _____ Starting & Ending Pages: _____
Article Title: _____
_____

2) Journal Title: _____
    Vol/Issue/Year: _____ Starting & Ending Pages: _____
Article Title: _____
_____

3) Journal Title: _____
    Vol/Issue/Year: _____ Starting & Ending Pages: _____
Article Title: _____
_____

4) Journal Title: _____
    Vol/Issue/Year: _____ Starting & Ending Pages: _____
Article Title: _____
_____

(See other side for Costs and Payment Information)

COSTS: Please figure your cost to order quality copies of an article.

1. Set-up charge per article: $8.00
   ($8.00 × number of separate articles)   _____

2. Photocopying charge for each article:

   1-10 pages: $1.00   _____

   11-19 pages: $3.00   _____

   20-29 pages: $5.00   _____

   30+ pages: $2.00/10 pages   _____

3. Flexicover (optional): $2.00/article   _____

4. Postage & Handling: US: $1.00 for the first article/
   $.50 each additional article   _____

   Federal Express: $25.00   _____

   Outside US: $2.00 for first article/
   $.50 each additional article _____

5. Same-day FAX service: $.35 per page   _____

GRAND TOTAL: _____

METHOD OF PAYMENT: (please check one)

❏ Check enclosed   ❏ Please ship and bill. PO # _____
(sorry we can ship and bill to bookstores only! All others must pre-pay)

❏ Charge to my credit card: ❏ Visa; ❏ MasterCard; ❏ Discover;
❏ American Express;

Account Number: _____   Expiration date: _____

Signature: ✗ _____

Name: _____   Institution: _____

Address: _____

_____

City: _____   State: _____   Zip: _____

Phone Number: _____   FAX Number: _____

MAIL or *FAX* THIS ENTIRE ORDER FORM TO:

Haworth Document Delivery Service   **or FAX:** 1-800-895-0582
The Haworth Press, Inc.   **or CALL:** 1-800-342-9678
10 Alice Street   9am-5pm EST)
Binghamton, NY 13904-1580